Rick

POCKET

AMSTERDAM

Rick Steves & Gene Openshaw

Contents

Introduction

Amsterdam of the golden age (the 1600s) was the world's richest city. And it's still a wonderland of canals, stately brick mansions, and carillons chiming from church spires. Today's Amsterdam is a progressive place of 850,000 people and almost as many bikes. Visitors will find no end of world-class sights: Van Gogh's Sunflowers, Rembrandt's self-portraits, and Anne Frank's secret hiding place.

Enjoy the city's intimate charms. Stroll quiet neighborhoods, browse bookshops, sample exotic foods, and let a local show you the right way to swallow a pickled herring. With legal marijuana and sex work, Amsterdam exudes an earthy spirit of live and let live. Consider yourself warned...or titillated. Take it all in, then pause to watch the clouds blow past gabled rooftops—and see the golden age reflected in a quiet canal.

Amsterdam

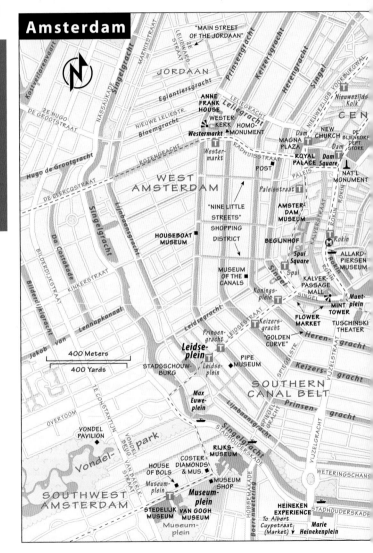

"MAIN STREET OF THE JORDAAN"

JORDAAN

Eglantiersgracht

ANNE FRANK HOUSE

Nieuwezijds Kolk

CEN

NEW CHURCH

DE BIJENKORF DEPT. STORE

WESTER-KERK

HOMO-MONUMENT

Westermarkt

Westermarkt

POST

Dam MAGNA PLAZA

ROYAL PALACE

Dam Square

NAT'L MONUMENT

WEST AMSTERDAM

Paleisstraat

"NINE LITTLE STREETS" SHOPPING DISTRICT

HOUSEBOAT MUSEUM

AMSTER-DAM MUSEUM

BEGIJNHOF

MUSEUM OF THE CANALS

Spui Square

Spui

ALLARD-PIERSEN MUSEUM

Koningsplein

KALVER-PASSAGE MALL

Muntplein

MINT TOWER

Leidsegracht

Prinsengracht

Keizersgracht

FLOWER MARKET

TUSCHINSKI THEATER

Leidseplein

"GOLDEN CURVE"

STADSSCHOUWBURG

Leidseplein

PIPE MUSEUM

SOUTHERN CANAL BELT

400 Meters

400 Yards

Max Euweplein

Prinsengracht

Keizersgracht

VONDEL PAVILION

Vondelpark

RIJKS-MUSEUM

Singelgracht

STADHOUDERSKADE

WETERINGSCHANS

SOUTHWEST AMSTERDAM

HOUSE OF BOLS

COSTER DIAMONDS & MUS.

MUSEUM SHOP

STEDELIJK MUSEUM

Museum-plein

VAN GOGH MUSEUM

HEINEKEN EXPERIENCE

To Albert Cuypstraat (Market)

Marie Heinekenplein

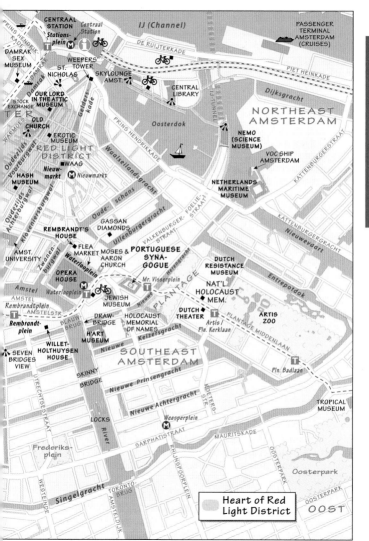

PRINS HENDRIK KADE

CENTRAAL STATION
Stationsplein

Centraal Station

IJ (Channel)

DE RUIJTERKADE

PASSENGER TERMINAL AMSTERDAM (CRUISES)

DAMRAK SEX MUSEUM

WEEPERS ST. TOWER NICHOLAS

SKYLOUNGE AMST.

CENTRAL LIBRARY

IJ-TUNNEL

PIET HEINKADE

Dijksgracht

OUR LORD IN THE ATTIC MUSEUM

Geldersekade

PRINS HENDRIKKADE

Oosterdok

NORTHEAST AMSTERDAM

KATTENBURGERSTRAAT

STOCK EXCHANGE

OLD CHURCH

EROTIC MUSEUM

NEMO (SCIENCE MUSEUM)

RED LIGHT DISTRICT

Waalseilandsgracht

VOC SHIP AMSTERDAM

Oudezijds Voorburgwal

Nieuwe markt

WAAG

Nieuwmarkt

NETHERLANDS MARITIME MUSEUM

KATTENBURGERGRACHT

HASH MUSEUM

Oudezijds Achterburgwal

Kloveniersburgwal

Oude schans

Nieuwevaart

REMBRANDT'S HOUSE

GASSAN DIAMONDS

Uilenburgergracht

AMST. UNIVERSITY

FLEA MARKET

MOSES & AARON CHURCH

VALKENBURGER-STRAAT

FOELIE-STRAAT

Zwanenburgwal

Waterlooplein

PORTUGESE SYNA-GOGUE

DUTCH RESISTANCE MUSEUM

Entrepotdok

OPERA HOUSE

Waterlooplein

Mr. Visserplein

NAT'L. HOLOCAUST MEM.

KATTENBURGERGRACHT

Amstel

JEWISH MUSEUM

PLANTAGE

ARTIS ZOO

Rembrandtplein

AMSTELSTR.

Rembrandt-plein

DRAW-BRIDGE

HOLOCAUST MEMORIAL OF NAMES

DUTCH THEATER

Artis / Pln. Kerklaan

PLANTAGE MIDDENLAAN

BLAUW-BRUG

H'ART MUSEUM

Keizersgracht

SEVEN BRIDGES VIEW

WILLET-HOLTHUYSEN HOUSE

SOUTHEAST AMSTERDAM

Pln. Badlaan

UTRECHTSESTRAAT

SKINNY BRIDGE

Nieuwe Prinsengracht

Nieuwe

KERKSTR.

Nieuwe Achtergracht

TROPICAL MUSEUM

LOCKS

River

Weesperplein

RHIJNSPOORPLEIN

Frederiks-plein

MAURITSKADE

OOSTERPARK

Oosterpark

WESTEINDE

Singelgracht

TORONTO-BRUG

AMSTELDIJK

SARPHATISTRAAT

OOSTERPARK

OOST

Heart of Red Light District

About This Book

Rick Steves Pocket Amsterdam is a personal tour guide...in your pocket. The core of the book is six self-guided walks and tours that zero in on Amsterdam's greatest sights and experiences. The Amsterdam City Walk takes you through the heart of the city, giving you the lay of the land. At the Rijksmuseum and Van Gogh Museum, you'll see all the essentials with time left over for browsing. You'll tour the racy Red Light District, meander the tree-lined canals of the Jordaan, and visit the tragic yet uplifting Anne Frank House.

The rest of this book is a traveler's tool kit, with my best advice on how to save money, plan your time, use public transportation, and avoid lines at the busiest sights. You'll also get recommendations on hotels, restaurants, and activities.

Amsterdam by Neighborhood

Amsterdam's Centraal station, on the north edge of the city, is your starting point, with trams branching out to all points. Damrak is the main north-south axis, connecting Centraal station with Dam Square and its Royal Palace. From this main street, the city spreads out like a fan, with 90 islands, hundreds of bridges, and a series of concentric canals that were laid out in the 17th century. Amsterdam's major sights are all within walking distance of Dam Square.

To the east of Damrak is the oldest part of the city (today's Red Light District), and to the west is the newer part, where you'll find the Anne Frank House and the peaceful Jordaan neighborhood. Museums and Leidseplein nightlife cluster at the southern edge of the city center.

Central Amsterdam—the historic core—runs from Centraal station south along Damrak, passing through two major city squares (Dam and Spui) and ending at the Mint Tower. Underfoot, the new North-South Metro line serves as a kind of underground Damrak, extending many miles in both directions.

West Amsterdam—from Dam Square to the Anne Frank House—is famous for its four grand canals that circle the historic core. With tree-lined canals fronted by old, gabled mansions, it's home to many of my recommended accommodations and restaurants. Within West Amsterdam is the boutique shopping district known as the Nine Little Streets. Farther west is the quieter, cozier Jordaan neighborhood. And to the north the old "Haarlem dike"—Haarlemmerstraat

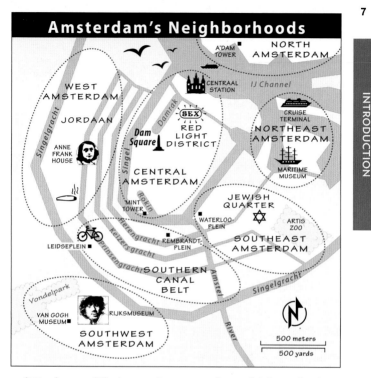

Amsterdam's Neighborhoods

(Map labels:)

NORTH AMSTERDAM

A'DAM TOWER

IJ Channel

CENTRAAL STATION

WEST AMSTERDAM

JORDAAN

Singelgracht

Damrak

SEX

RED LIGHT DISTRICT

Dam Square

CRUISE TERMINAL

NORTHEAST AMSTERDAM

MARITIME MUSEUM

ANNE FRANK HOUSE

Singel

CENTRAL AMSTERDAM

JEWISH QUARTER

'MINT TOWER

Rokin

WATERLOO-PLEIN

ARTIS ZOO

Herengracht

REMBRANDT-PLEIN

SOUTHEAST AMSTERDAM

Keizersgracht

LEIDSEPLEIN

Prinsengracht

SOUTHERN CANAL BELT

Amstel

Singelgracht

Vondelpark

VAN GOGH MUSEUM

RIJKSMUSEUM

SOUTHWEST AMSTERDAM

River

N

500 meters
500 yards

and Haarlemmerdijk—is emerging as a trendy, youthful zone for shopping and eating.

The **Southern Canal Belt**—the next ring of canals south of the historic core—is spacious and dotted sparsely with a few intimate museums, art galleries, and antique shops along Nieuwe Spiegelstraat. Rowdy Leidseplein anchors the lower corner.

Southwest Amsterdam is defined by two main features: museums and a city park. The city's major art museums (Rijksmuseum, Van Gogh, and Stedelijk) and other sights cluster together on an expansive square, Museumplein. The museums are just a short walk from Vondelpark, Amsterdam's "central park."

Southeast Amsterdam contains the former Jewish Quarter

Amsterdam at a Glance

▲▲▲**Rijksmuseum** Best collection anywhere of the Dutch Masters—Rembrandt, Hals, Vermeer, and Steen—in a spectacular setting. **Hours:** Daily 9:00-17:00. See page 37.

▲▲▲**Van Gogh Museum** More than 200 paintings by the angst-ridden artist. **Hours:** Daily 9:00-17:00, may stay open later in summer, shorter hours off-season. See page 57.

▲▲▲**Anne Frank House** Young Anne's hideaway during the Nazi occupation. **Hours:** Daily 9:00-22:00. See page 107.

▲▲**Stedelijk Museum** The Netherlands' top modern-art museum. **Hours:** Daily 10:00-18:00. See page 125.

▲▲**Amsterdam Museum** City's growth from fishing village to trading capital to today, including some Rembrandts and a playable carillon. **Hours:** Closed for renovation. See page 28.

▲▲**Red Light District** The world's oldest profession in the city's oldest neighborhood. **Hours:** Best from noon into the evening; avoid late at night. See page 73.

▲▲**Our Lord in the Attic Museum** Catholic church hidden in the attic of a 17th-century merchant's house. **Hours:** Mon-Fri 10:00-17:00, Sat until 18:00, Sun 13:00-18:00. See page 133.

▲▲**Netherlands Maritime Museum** Rich seafaring story of the Netherlands, told with vivid artifacts. **Hours:** Daily 10:00-17:00, closed Mon off-season. See page 134.

▲▲**Dutch Resistance Museum** History of the Dutch struggle against the Nazis. **Hours:** Mon-Fri 10:00-17:00, Sat-Sun from 11:00. See page 139.

and the Jewish Museum. Several sights can be found around the square known as Waterlooplein (Rembrandt's House and a flea market). Additional sights are gathered in a park-dotted area called the Plantage (Dutch Resistance Museum, a theater-turned-Holocaust-memorial, a zoo, and a botanical garden). Rembrandtplein, another nightlife center, is a five-minute walk away.

Northeast Amsterdam has the Netherlands Maritime Museum,

▲**Royal Palace** Lavish City Hall that takes you back to the golden age of the 17th century. **Hours:** Daily 10:00-17:00 when not closed for official ceremonies. See page 23.

▲**Begijnhof** Quiet courtyard lined with picturesque houses. **Hours:** Daily 10:00-18:00. See page 28.

▲**Hash, Marijuana, and Hemp Museum** All the dope, from history and science to memorabilia. **Hours:** Daily 10:00-22:00. See page 89.

▲**A'dam Tower** Entertainment complex with panoramic views over Amsterdam. **Hours:** Daily 10:00-22:00. See page 135.

▲**Rembrandt's House** The master's reconstructed house, displaying his etchings. **Hours:** Tue-Sun 10:00-18:00, closed Mon. See page 135.

▲**Willet-Holthuysen House** Elegant 17th-century house. **Hours:** Daily 10:00-17:00. See page 127.

▲**Jewish Museum and Portuguese Synagogue** Exhibits on Judaism and culture and beloved synagogue that serves today's Jewish community. **Hours:** Museum daily 10:00-17:00; synagogue Sun-Fri 10:00-17:00, closes earlier Dec-Jan and Fri off-season, closed Sat year-round. See page 137.

▲**Dutch Theater** Moving memorial in former Jewish detention center. **Hours:** Daily 11:00-17:00. See page 138.

▲**Tropical Museum** Large ethnographic collection exploring Dutch colonialism. **Hours:** Daily 10:00-17:00, closed Mon off-season. See page 140.

Amsterdam's Central Library, and a children's science museum (NEMO).

North Amsterdam sits across the very wide IJ (pronounced "eye") waterway. Long neglected as a sleepy residential zone, recently it has sprouted interesting restaurant and nightlife options, thanks to the construction of the EYE Filmmuseum, the A'dam Tower, and a new North-South subway connection to the center.

Planning Your Time

Amsterdam is worth a full day on even the busiest itinerary and can easily fill three full sightseeing days. The following day plans give an idea of how much an organized, motivated, and caffeinated person can see. Note that tickets for the Van Gogh Museum, the Rijksmuseum, and the Anne Frank House must all be reserved online in advance (see those chapters for details).

Day 1: Follow my self-guided Amsterdam City Walk from the train station to Spui, with stops at Dam Square, the peaceful Begijnhof, and the flower market. After lunch, visit Amsterdam's two great art museums, located side by side: the Van Gogh Museum and the Rijksmuseum. In the evening, stroll the Red Light District for some fascinating window-shopping.

Day 2: Start your day with a one-hour canal boat tour. Then visit the sights of your choice around Rembrandtplein (Rembrandt's House, Waterlooplein flea market, Gassan Diamonds polishing demo, Dutch Resistance Museum). In the late afternoon, tour the Anne Frank House, then take my self-guided Jordaan Walk before enjoying dinner in that neighborhood.

Day 3: Use this day to browse your choice of Amsterdam's more than 50 museums, such as Our Lord in the Attic, Royal Palace, Stedelijk, Pipe, and Houseboat.

With More Time: There are plenty of other small museums in Amsterdam—find suggestions in the Sights chapter. Or day-trip to nearby towns such as Haarlem, Delft, or Edam.

When to Go

Although Amsterdam can be crowded in summer, it's a great time to

The Begijnhof—peaceful oasis in the city

Flower markets burst with color and scents.

visit, with long days, lively festivals, and sunny weather (rarely too hot for comfort, extremely long hours of daylight).

Amsterdam can also be busy—and hotel prices higher—in late March, April, and May, when the tulip fields are in full bloom. Fall comes with lighter crowds, though conferences can drive up prices. Spring and fall generally have mild weather. Amsterdam in winter (late Oct-mid-March) is cold and wet, but the city feels lively, not touristy.

Before You Go

You'll have a smoother trip if you tackle a few things ahead of time. For more details on these topics, see the Practicalities chapter and RickSteves.com, which has helpful travel-tip articles and videos.

Make sure your travel documents are valid. If your passport is due to expire within six months of your ticketed date of return, you need to renew it. Allow 12 weeks or more to renew or get a passport. Be aware of any entry requirements; you may need to register with the European Travel Information and Authorization System (ETIAS) before you travel (quick and easy process; check https://travel-europe. europa.eu/etias_en). Get passport and country-specific travel info at Travel.State.gov.

Arrange your transportation. Book your international flights. If traveling beyond Amsterdam, research train reservations, rail passes, and car rentals.

Book rooms well in advance, especially if your trip falls during peak season or any major holidays or festivals.

Reserve ahead for key sights. At some Amsterdam sights—the Rijksmuseum, Van Gogh Museum, and Anne Frank House—advance reservations are required (even with a sightseeing pass). Because tickets often sell out for the Anne Frank House, buy them six weeks before your visit (when tickets go on sale). More details are in each tour chapter.

Consider travel insurance. Compare the cost of insurance to the cost of your potential loss. Understand what protections your credit card might offer and whether your existing insurance (health, homeowners, or renters) covers you and your possessions overseas.

Manage your money. "Tap-to-pay" or "contactless" cards are widely accepted and simple to use. You may need your credit card's PIN for some purchases—request it if you don't have one. Alert your

INTRODUCTION

Rick's Free Audio Tours and Video Clips

Rick Steves Audio Europe, a free app, makes it easy to download my audio tours and listen to them offline as you travel. For this book (look for the 🎧), free audio tours cover my Amsterdam City Walk, Jordaan Walk, and Red Light District Walk. The app also offers my public radio show interviews with travel experts from around the globe. Scan the QR code on the inside front cover to find it in your app store, or visit RickSteves.com/AudioEurope.

    Rick Steves Classroom Europe, a powerful tool for teachers, is also useful for travelers. This video library contains about 600 short clips excerpted from my public television series. Enjoy these videos as you sort through options for your trip and to better understand what you'll see in Europe. Check it out at Classroom.RickSteves.com.

bank that you'll be using your debit and credit cards in Europe. You don't need to bring euros; you can withdraw euros from ATMs in Europe.

    Use your smartphone smartly. Sign up for an international service plan to reduce your costs, or rely on Wi-Fi in Europe instead. Download any apps you'll want on the road, such as maps, translators, and Rick Steves Audio Europe (see sidebar).

    Pack light. You'll walk with your luggage more than you think. I travel for weeks with a single carry-on bag and a day pack. Use the packing checklist in Practicalities as a guide.

Travel Smart

If you have a positive attitude, equip yourself with good information (this book), and expect to travel smart, you will.

    Pickpockets abound in crowded places where tourists congregate. Treat commotions as smokescreens for theft. Keep your passport and backup cash and credit cards secure in a money belt tucked under your clothes; carry only a day's spending money and a card in your front pocket or wallet.

If you wilt easily, choose a hotel with air-conditioning, start your day early, take a midday siesta, and resume your sightseeing later.

Be sure to schedule in slack time for picnics, laundry, people-watching, leisurely dinners, shopping, and recharging your touristic batteries. Slow down and be open to unexpected experiences and the hospitality of the Amsterdammers.

Learn how to eat herring like a local, bump along on a bike over cobblestones, or slowly nurse a drink in a brown café. As you visit places I know and love, I'm happy you'll be meeting some of my favorite Dutch people.

Happy travels! *Goede vakantie!*

Amsterdam City Walk

From Centraal Station to Leidseplein

Take a Dutch sampler walk from one end of the old center to the other, tasting all that Amsterdam has to offer along the way. It's your best single stroll through quintessentially Dutch scenes, hidden churches, surprising shops, thriving happy-hour hangouts, and eight centuries of history.

The walk starts at Centraal station, heads down touristy Damrak to Dam Square, and continues south down pedestrian-only Kalverstraat to the Mint Tower. Then it wafts through the flower market, before dropping by the herring stand on Koningsplein and circling back to Spui Square. To return to Centraal station, catch trams #2 or #12 from Spui Square.

ORIENTATION

Length of This Walk: Allow about two hours.

When to Go: Best during the day, when sights are open.

Alert: Beware of silent transport—trams and bikes. Walkers should stay off the tram tracks and bike paths, and yield to bell-ringing bikers.

Royal Palace: €12.50, daily 10:00-17:00 but hours can vary for official business.

New Church: €9-16 to enter interior (depending on special exhibits), daily 10:00-18:00.

De Papegaai Hidden Church: Free, Mon-Sat 10:00-16:00, Sun until 13:30.

Amsterdam Museum: Typically a highlight of this walk, this wonderful museum is now closed for a major renovation.

Begijnhof: Free, daily 10:00-18:00.

Tours: 🎧 Download my free Amsterdam City Walk audio tour.

Services: You can find WCs at fast-food places and in the Kalvertoren shopping mall.

THE WALK BEGINS

❶ Centraal Station

Here, where today's train travelers enter the city, sailors of yore disembarked from seagoing ships. They were met by street musicians, pickpockets, hotel runners, and ladies carrying red lanterns. Centraal station, built in the late 1800s, sits on reclaimed land at what was once the harbor mouth. With warm red brick and prickly spires, the station is the first of several Neo-Gothic buildings we'll see from the late 19th century, the era of Amsterdam's economic revival. One of the station's towers has a clock dial; the other tower's dial is a weather vane. Watch the hand twitch as the wind gusts in every direction—N, Z, O, and W.

Let's get oriented: *nord, zuid, ost,* and *vest.* Facing the station, you're facing north. Farther north, on the other side of the station, is the IJ (pronounced "eye"), the body of water that gives Amsterdam access to the open sea.

Now turn your back to the station and face the city, looking south. The city spreads out before you like a fan, in a series of concentric canals. Ahead of you stretches the street called Damrak, which leads—like a red carpet for guests entering Amsterdam—to Dam Square a half-mile away. That's where we're headed.

To the left of Damrak is the city's old (*oude*) town. The crown-topped steeple of the Old Church (Oude Kerk) marks the center of that neighborhood. That historic quarter has long been the Red Light District (□ see the Red Light District Walk chapter). Closer to you, towering above the old part of town, is the domed St. Nicholas Church. It was built in the 1880s, when Catholics—after about three centuries of oppression—were finally free to worship in public. To your far left is the DoubleTree by Hilton Hotel, with its 11th-floor SkyLounge Amsterdam offering perhaps the city's best viewpoint.

To the right of Damrak is the new (*nieuwe*) part of town, where you'll find the Anne Frank House and the peaceful Jordaan neighborhood.

The train station is the city's transportation center. Many trams leave from out front. Beneath your feet is a new Metro line. In the "Golden 1990s," when the economy was booming, Amsterdam committed the city to a grand infrastructure expansion to accommodate the tens of thousands of people living in North Amsterdam, the fast-growing suburb beyond the IJ. Today this plaza, while providing a people-friendly welcome to the city, also works as an efficient transit hub.

On your far right, in front of Ibis Hotel, is a huge, multistory **parking garage**—for bikes only. Biking in Holland is the way to go—the land is flat, distances are short, and there are designated bike paths everywhere. The bike parking garage is free, courtesy of the

Centraal Station, the city's transit hub

Bikes—and bike lanes—are everywhere.

government, and intended to encourage this green and ultra-efficient mode of transportation.

▶ *Let's head out. With your back to the station, start walking south into the city to the head of Damrak. Be aware of trams and bikes as you cross the street. Keep going south straight along the right side of the street, following the crowds on...*

❷ Damrak

This street was once a riverbank. It's where the Amstel River flowed north into the IJ, which led to a vast inlet of the North Sea called the Zuiderzee. It's this unique geography that turned Amsterdam into a center of trade. Boats could sail up the Amstel into the interior of Europe, or out to the North Sea, to reach the rest of the world.

As you stroll along Damrak, look left. There's a marina, lined with old brick buildings. Though they aren't terribly historic, the scene still captures a bit of golden age Amsterdam. Think of it: Back in the 1600s, this area was the harbor, and those buildings warehoused exotic goods from all over the world.

All along Damrak, you'll pass a veritable gauntlet of touristy shops. These seem to cover every Dutch cliché. You'll see wooden shoes, which the Dutch used to wear to get around easily in the marshy soil, and all manner of tulips; the real ones come from Holland's famed fresh-flower industry. Heineken fridge magnets advertise one of the world's most popular pilsner beers. There are wheels of cheese, marijuana-leaf hats, team jerseys for the Ajax football (soccer) club, and memorabilia with the city's "XXX" logo. You'll likely hear a hand-cranked barrel organ and see windmill-shaped saltshakers. And everything seems to be available in bright orange—the official color of the Dutch royal family.

At the **Damrak Sex Museum** at Damrak 18, you'll find the city's most notorious commodity on display. As a port town catering to sailors and businessmen away from home, Amsterdam has always accommodated the sex trade. Continue up Damrak. You'll pass places selling the popular local fast food: french fries. Here they're called **Vlaamse friets**—Flemish fries—since they were invented in the Low Countries. The stand at Damrak 41 is a favorite, where plenty of locals stop to dip their fries in mayonnaise (not ketchup).

Farther up Damrak, you'll pass many restaurants. It quickly becomes obvious that, here, international cuisine is almost like going local. Restaurants serving **rijsttafel,** a sampler of assorted Indonesian dishes, are especially popular, thanks to the days when the Dutch East Indies were a colony. Amsterdammers on the go often grab a simple sandwich (*broodje*) or a pita-bread wrap (*shoarma*) from a Middle Eastern takeout joint.

Remember, we're walking along what was once the Amstel River. Today, the Amstel is channeled into canals and its former mouth is covered by Centraal station. But Amsterdam still remains a major seaport. That's because, in the 19th century, the Dutch dug the North Sea Canal to create a shorter route to the open sea. These days, more than 100,000 ships a year dock on the outskirts of Amsterdam, making it Europe's fourth-busiest seaport (giant cruise ships stop here as well). For all of Amsterdam's existence, it's been a trading center.

▶ *The long brick building with the square clock tower, along the left side of Damrak, is the...*

❸ Stock Exchange (Beurs van Berlage)

This impressive structure, a symbol of the city's long tradition as a trading town, was built with nine million bricks. Like so many buildings in this once-marshy city, it was constructed on a foundation of pilings—some 5,000 tree trunks hammered vertically into the soil. When the Beurs opened in 1903, it was one of the world's first modernist buildings, with a geometric, minimal, no-frills style. Emphasizing function over looks, it helped set the architectural tone for many 20th-century buildings. Note how the reliefs celebrate the worker—it was a time of "capitalism with a heart" (free trade but with a greater respect for workers).

Make your way to the end of the long, century-old building. Amsterdammers have gathered in this neighborhood to trade since medieval times. Back then, "trading stock" meant buying and selling goats, chickens, or kegs of beer. Over time, they began exchanging slips of paper, or "futures," rather than actual goods. Traders needed moneychangers, who needed bankers, who made money by lending money. By the 1600s, Amsterdam had become one of the world's first great capitalist cities, loaning money to free-spending kings, dukes, and bishops.

When you reach the end of the building, look across the square called **Beursplein.** In 1984, the Beurs building was turned into a cultural center, and the stock exchange moved next door to the Euronext

Amsterdam City Walk

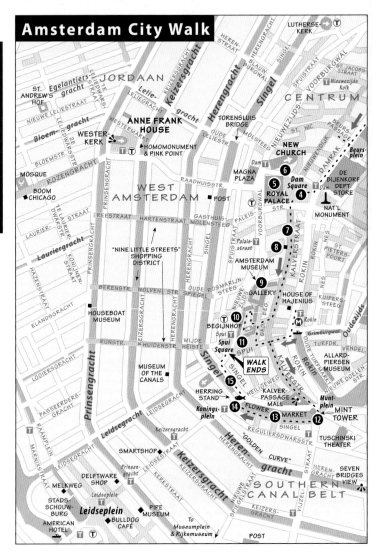

1 Centraal Station
2 Damrak
3 Stock Exchange (Beurs)
4 Dam Square
5 Royal Palace
6 New Church
7 Kalverstraat
8 De Papegaai Hidden Church
9 Amsterdam Museum
10 Begijnhof
11 Spui Square
12 Mint Tower
13 Flower Market
14 Koningsplein and a Herring Stand
15 Koningsplein to Spui

Heart of Red Light District

200 Meters
200 Yards

complex. See the stock price readout board. How's your Heineken stock doing? Amsterdam still thrives as the center of Dutch business and, besides Heineken, is home to Shell Oil, Philips Electronics, and ING Bank.

Directly opposite Beursplein on Damrak (at #68) is **Beurspassage,** a fancy, faux Art Nouveau shopping passageway. Use the crosswalk and enter the passage. Wander down and back to notice the symbols of the city. Fill your water bottle in the mouth of a fish. Enjoy the marble floor, the chandeliers and Tiffany lanterns, and the mosaic ceiling depicting a primordial soup with all the stuff you'd find tossed into a canal, from old bike tires to Van Gogh's ear.

▶ *Continue up Damrak until it opens into Dam Square. Make your way—carefully—across the street to the cobblestone pavement. Stand in the middle of the square and take it all in.*

❹ Dam Square

This is the historic heart of Amsterdam. The city got its start right here in about the year 1250, when fishermen in this marshy delta settled along the built-up banks of the Amstel River. They built a *damme,* blocking the Amstel River, and creating a small village called "Amsteldamme." To the north was the *damrak* ("outer harbor"), a waterway that led to the sea. That's the street we just walked. To the south was the *rokin* ("inner harbor"), for river traffic inland. Fishermen were soon trading with German riverboats traveling downstream and with seafaring boats from Stockholm, Hamburg, and London. Dam Square was the center of it all.

Today, Dam Square is still the center of Dutch life, at least symbolically. The Royal Palace and major department stores face the square. Mimes, jugglers, and human statues mingle with locals and tourists. As Holland's most recognizable square, this is where political demonstrations begin and end.

Circling the Square: Pan the square clockwise and take in the sights, starting with the Royal Palace—the large domed building on the west side. To its right stands the New Church (Nieuwe Kerk). Panning past Damrak, see the proud old De Bijenkorf ("The Beehive") department store (with a view café).

Farther right, the Grand Hotel Krasnapolsky has a lovely circa-1900 glass-roofed "winter garden." The white obelisk is the National Monument, built in 1956 to honor WWII casualties. When

Dam Square, with its WWII memorial, is the symbolic center of the Netherlands.

the Nazis occupied Holland from 1940 to 1945, they deported some 60,000 Jewish Amsterdammers, driving many—including young Anne Frank and her family—into hiding. The "Hunger Winter" of 1944-1945 killed thousands of Dutch and forced many to survive on little more than tulip bulbs. This obelisk—with its carvings of the crucified Christ, men in chains, and howling dogs—remembers the suffering of that grim time and is also considered a monument for peace. A few blocks behind the hotel is the edge of the Red Light District. To the right of the hotel stretches the street called the Nes, lined with some of Amsterdam's edgy live-theater venues. Panning farther right, find Rokin street—Damrak's southern counterpart. Next, just to the right of the touristy Madame Tussauds, is Kalverstraat, a busy pedestrian-only shopping street.

❺ Royal Palace (Koninklijk Huis)

Despite the name, this is really the former City Hall. In medieval times, this was where the city council and mayor met. Amsterdam was a self-governing community that prided itself on its independence and thumbed its nose at royalty. In about 1650, the old medieval Town Hall was replaced with this one. Its style is appropriately Classical, recalling the democratic Greeks. (That's a nice message, but the government

Amsterdam's Story

Beginnings: Situated at the mouth of the Amstel River, Amsterdam was where Rhine riverboats met sea-going vessels—trade flourished. Around 1250, locals built a dam on the Amstel, creating "Amstel-dam." They drained the marshy delta, channeled the water into canals, sank pilings, and built a city from scratch.

1300s Charter: Amsterdam was already an international trade center for German beer, locally caught herring, cloth, bacon, salt, and wine. When the region's leading bishop granted the town a charter (1300), Amsterdammers could then set up law courts, judge their own matters, and be essentially autonomous.

1500s Growth: Amsterdam became a bustling trade-and-banking center of 12,000 people crammed within the Singel canal. The walled city was ruled from afar by Catholic Habsburgs in Spain. Angry Protestants rose up, vandalizing Catholic churches and starting a war of independence (officially granted in 1648).

1600s Golden Age: Meanwhile, Holland was inventing the global economy. In 1602, hardy Dutch sailors (and Henry Hudson, an Englishman in Dutch service) tried their hand at trade with the Far East. When they returned, they brought with them valuable spices, diamonds, rijsttafel recipes...and the golden age. The Dutch East India Company (abbreviated "VOC" in Dutch), a state-subsidized import/export business,

combined nautical skills with capitalist investing. With 500 or so 150-foot ships cruising in and out of Amsterdam's harbor, it was the first great multinational corporation.

Golden age Amsterdam (pop. 100,000) was perhaps the wealthiest city on earth—the "warehouse of the world." Goods came from everywhere. The VOC's specialties were spices (pepper and cinnamon), coffee and tea, Chinese porcelain, and silk. Meanwhile, the competing Dutch West India Company concentrated on the New World, trading enslaved African people for South American sugar. With its wealth, the city expanded west and south, adding new canals lined with gabled mansions. Rembrandt, Vermeer, and Hals captured the can-do spirit on canvas.

At the peak of the golden age, Amsterdam was gripped by "tulip mania." Investors drove the value of tulip bulbs to insane heights. Then, in 1637, the market crashed, symbolically marking the end of an era. Soon, Holland was eclipsed by new superpowers England and France, which took over the overseas trade and scuttled their fleet in demoralizing wars.

1700s Decline: Amsterdam became a city of backwater bankers and small manufacturers—still a cultural center but befitting Holland's small size. The city hit rock bottom in 1795: French troops invaded, and proud Holland was soon saddled with a monarchy.

1800s Revival: The tech-minded Dutch built a canal to the North Sea, rejuvenating Amsterdam's port. Railroads laced the country, and Amsterdam expanded southward by draining new land. The Rijksmuseum, Centraal station, and Magna Plaza (formerly the main post office) date from this economic upswing.

1900s: The 1930s Depression hit hard, followed by five years of occupation under the Nazis, aided by pro-Nazi Dutch. The city's large Jewish population was decimated by Nazi deportations and extermination (falling from about 75,000 Jews in 1940 to just 15,000 in 1945). With postwar prosperity, 1960s Amsterdam became a global center for Europe's hippies, promoting legal marijuana, free sex, and free bikes.

Today: Amsterdam is now a city of 850,000 people jammed into small apartments (often with the same floor plan as their neighbors'). Since the 1970s, many immigrants have become locals. One in 10 Amsterdammers is Surinamese, and one in 10 prays toward Mecca.

City on a Sandbar

Amsterdam sits in the marshy delta at the mouth of the Amstel River—a completely man-made city, built on millions of wooden pilings. (The wood survives if kept wet and out of the air.) Since World War II, concrete has been used for the pilings, with foundations driven 60 feet deep through a layer of sand, then mud, and into a second layer of sand. Today's biggest buildings have foundations that go down as far as 120 feet. Yet, many of the city's buildings tend to lean this way and that as their pilings settle.

was really more like an oligarchy, ruled by rich and powerful trading families.) The triangular pediment features denizens of the sea cavorting with Neptune and his gilded copper trident—all appropriate imagery for sea-trading Amsterdam. The small balcony (just above the entry doors) is where city leaders have long appeared for major speeches, pronouncements, executions, and (these days) for newly married royalty to blow kisses to the crowds.

Today, the palace remains one of the four official residences of King Willem-Alexander and is usually open to visitors (see page 129).

▶ *A few paces away, to the right as you're facing the Royal Palace, is the...*

❻ New Church (Nieuwe Kerk)

Though called the "New" Church, this building is actually 600 years old—a mere 100 years newer than the "Old" Church (in the Red Light District). The sundial above the entrance once served as the city's official timepiece.

This church is where many of the Netherlands' monarchs are married, and all are "inaugurated." (Dutch royals are not crowned, as they never actually wear the official crown.) If you pay the expensive fee to go inside, you'll see a spacious, well-lit, yet bare interior (occupied by a new art exhibit every three months) that looks quite different from the Baroque-encrusted churches found in the rest of Europe.

In 1566, clear-eyed Protestant extremists throughout Holland marched into Catholic churches (including this one), lopped off the heads of holy statues, stripped gold-leaf angels from the walls, urinated on Virgin Marys, and shattered stained-glass windows in a wave of anti-Catholic vandalism.

Royal Palace on Dam Square

New Church, where royals marry

This iconoclasm (icon-breaking) of 1566 started an 80-year war against Spain and the Habsburgs, leading finally to Dutch independence in 1648. Catholic churches like this one were converted to the new dominant religion, Calvinist Protestantism (today's Dutch Reformed Church). From then on, Dutch churches downplayed the "graven images" and "idols" of ornate religious art.

▸ *From Dam Square, head south (going down the pedestrian mall just to the right of Madame Tussaud's).*

❼ Kalverstraat

Kalverstraat (strictly pedestrian-only—even bikers need to dismount and walk) has been a traditional shopping street for centuries. But today it's notorious among locals as a noisy, soulless string of chain stores. For smaller and more elegant stores, try the adjacent district called De Negen Straatjes ("The Nine Little Streets"). Only about four blocks west of Kalverstraat, it's where 200 or so shops and cafés mingle along tranquil canals.

▸ *About 100 yards along, keep a sharp eye out for the next sight (it's fairly easy to miss): On the right, just before and across from the Mc-Donald's, at #58, is...*

❽ De Papegaai Hidden Church (Petrus en Paulus Kerk)

This Catholic church is an oasis of peace amid crass 21st-century commercialism. It's not exactly a hidden church (after all, you've found it), but it still keeps a low profile, as it dates from an era when Catholics in Amsterdam were forced to worship in secret.

In the 1500s, Protestants were fighting Catholics all over Europe. For the next two centuries, Amsterdam's Catholics were driven

underground. While technically illegal here, Catholicism was tolerated. Catholics could worship so long as they practiced in humble,
unadvertised places, like this church. The church gets its nickname
from a parrot (*papegaai*) carved over the entrance of the house that
formerly stood on this site. Now, a stuffed parrot hangs in the nave to
remember that original *papegaai*.

▶ *Return to Kalverstraat and continue south for about 100 yards. At
#92, where Kalverstraat crosses Wijde Kapel Steeg, look to the right to
find an archway that leads to the...*

❾ Amsterdam Museum

The ▲▲ Amsterdam Museum—the city's history museum—is just
through this door, but it's closed for several years for a major renovation. Also closed is the museum's public corridor, the Amsterdam
Gallery (formerly known as the "Civic Guards Gallery"), lined with
group portraits of Amsterdam's citizens from the golden age to modern times.

Pause at the entrance to the museum complex to view the archway. On the slumping arch is Amsterdam's coat of arms—a red shield
with three Xs and a crown. The X-shaped crosses represent the crucifixion of St. Andrew, the patron saint of fishermen. Below that is a
relief (dated 1581) showing boys around a dove, asking for charity, reminding all who pass that this building was once an orphanage.

▶ *Continue down Kalverstraat to #128 from where a small lane on the
right, Begijnensteeg, leads directly to the old door of the Begijnhof.
(Admission into this sweet little haven is free but limited to 50 people
at a time.)*

❿ Begijnhof

This quiet courtyard, lined with houses around a church, has shel-
tered women since 1346. For centuries this was the home of a community of Beguines—pious and simple women who removed themselves
from the world at large to dedicate their lives to God.

As you enter, keep in mind that this spot isn't just a tourist attraction; it's also a place where people live. Be considerate: Don't photo-
graph the residents or their homes, be quiet, and stick to the area near
the churches.

Begin your visit by walking to the far end and find the **statue** of one of these charitable sisters. You'll find it just beyond the church. The Beguines' ranks swelled during the Crusades, when so many men took off, never to return. Later, women widowed by the hazards of overseas trade lived out their days as Beguines. Poor and rich women alike turned their backs on materialism and marriage to live here in Christian poverty. They spent their days deep in prayer and busy with daily tasks—spinning wool, making lace, teaching, and caring for the sick.

The statue of the Beguine faces a black **wooden house,** at #34. This structure dates from 1528 and is the city's oldest. Originally, the whole city consisted of wooden houses like this one. They were eventually replaced with brick houses to minimize the fire danger of so many homes packed together.

Now turn your attention to the brick-faced **English Reformed church** (Engelse Kerk), built in 1420 to serve the Beguine community. In 1607, this church became Anglican. It served as a refuge for English traders and religious separatists fleeing persecution in England. Strict Protestants such as the famous Pilgrims found sanctuary in tolerant Amsterdam and may have worshipped in this church. If the church is open, step inside, grab an English info sheet, and head to the far end, toward the stained-glass window. It shows the Pilgrims praying before boarding the *Mayflower*. Along the right-hand wall is an old pew (with columns and clock) they may have sat on, and on the altar is a Bible from 1763, with lot*f* of old-*f*tyle *f*'s. Also of note is the front pulpit, carved of wood. It's by Piet Mondrian, the famous Dutch abstract artist, and was one of his first professional gigs.

Back outside, find the **Catholic church,** which faces the English

Begijnhof—quiet courtyard for lay sisters

Beautiful interior of the "hidden" Catholic church

Reformed church. Because Catholics were being persecuted when it was built, this had to be a low-profile, "hidden" church—notice the painted-out windows on the second and third floors. Step inside, through the low-profile doorway. It's decorated lovingly, if on the cheap (try tapping softly on a "marble" column). Amsterdam's Catholics must have eagerly awaited the day when they were legally allowed to say Mass (that day finally came in the 19th century).

Today, Holland still has something of a religious divide, but not a bitter one. Amsterdam itself is pretty un-churched. But the Dutch countryside is much more religious, including a "Bible Belt" region where 98 percent of the population is Protestant. Overall, in the Netherlands, the country is divided fairly evenly between Catholics, Protestants, and those who see Sunday as a day to sleep in and enjoy a lazy brunch.

Step back outside. The last Beguine died in 1971, but this Begijnhof still thrives, providing subsidized housing to about 100 single women (mostly Catholic seniors). The Begijnhof is just one of a few dozen *hofjes* (little housing projects surrounding courtyards) that dot Amsterdam.

▶ *Leave the way you entered, turn right, and head for a leafy, cobbled square.*

⓫ Spui Square

Lined with cafés and bars, this square is one of the city's more popular spots for nightlife and sunny afternoon people-watching. Its name, Spui (rhymes with "now" and means "spew"), recalls the days when water was moved over dikes to keep the place dry.

We'll finish our walk at the far-right end of this square. But for now, head two blocks to the left, crossing busy Kalverstraat, to the bustling street called the **Rokin.** Across Rokin you can see the entry to the new North-South Metro line and a small black statue of Queen Wilhelmina daintily riding sidesaddle. Remember that in real life, she was the iron-willed inspiration for the Dutch resistance against the Nazis.

Turn left on the Rokin and walk up 50 yards to the **House of Hajenius** (at Rokin 92). This temple of cigars is a "paradise for the connoisseur," showing "175 years of tradition and good taste." Don't be shy—the place is as much a free museum for visitors as it is a store for paying customers.

From Hajenius, backtrack to the busy pedestrian mall, Kalverstraat, and continue south. Just before the end of this shopping boulevard (at #206, on the right), you'll see the modern Kalverpassage and the **Kalvertoren** shopping mall. Enter and go deeper within to find a slanting glass elevator. You can ride this to the recommended top-floor **Blue Amsterdam Restaurant,** where a coffee or light lunch buys you something that's rare in altitude-challenged Amsterdam—a nice view.

▶ *Back out on the street, at the end of Kalverstraat, stands the...*

⓬ Mint Tower (Munttoren)

This tower marked the limit of the medieval walled city and served as one of its original gates. In the Middle Ages, the city walls were girdled by a moat—the Singel canal. Until about 1500, the area beyond here was nothing but marshy fields and a few farms on reclaimed land. The Mint Tower's steeple was added later—in the year 1620, as you can see written below the clock face.

Today, the tower is a favorite within Amsterdam's marijuana culture. Stoners love to take a photo of the clock and its 1620 sign at exactly 4:20 p.m.—the traditional time to quit work and light one up. (On the 24-hour clock, 4:20 p.m. is 16:20...Du-u-u-ude!)

▶ *Continue past the Mint Tower, first walking a few yards south along busy Vijzelstraat (keep an eye out for trams). Then turn right and walk west along the south bank of the Singel canal. It's lined with the greenhouse shops of the...*

⓭ Flower Market (Bloemenmarkt)

The stands along this busy block sell cut flowers, plants, bulbs, seeds, garden supplies, and flower-oriented souvenirs and knickknacks. Browse your way along while heading for the end of the block.

The Flower Market is a testament to Holland's longtime love affair with flowers. The Netherlands is by far the largest flower exporter in Europe and a major flower power worldwide. If you're looking for a souvenir, note that certain seeds are marked as OK to bring back through customs into the US.

The best-known Dutch flower, the tulip, was brought from

The Mint Tower once marked the border of the medieval, walled city.

"Tulip mania" lives on at the Flower Market.

Be daring—try a herring.

central Asia in the mid-1500s. The hardy bulbs thrived in the sandy soil of Holland's reclaimed land. Within a generation, tulips grew from a trendy fad into an all-out frenzy. Soon, a single prized bulb could sell for the equivalent of thousands of dollars. By 1636, it was full-blown "Tulip mania"—yes, that's what the Dutch called it. Then in 1637 the tulip bubble burst. Overnight, once-wealthy investors were broke. The crash was devastating, and played a role in the decline of the golden age. But Holland's love of this delightful flower has lived on. Today, tulips are a major export, and are firmly planted in the Dutch psyche.

▶ *The long Flower Market ends at the next bridge, where you'll enter a square named Koningsplein (King's Square), with a characteristic herring shop.*

⑭ Koningsplein and a Herring Stand

Pleasant Koningsplein square hosts the popular **Frens Haringhandel** outdoor *haringhandel* (herring stand). This is a great place to choke down a raw herring—a fish that has a special place in every Dutch heart. After all, herring was the commodity that first put Amsterdam on the trading map. It's also what Dutch sailors ate for protein on those long cross-global voyages.

Throughout the Netherlands, old-fashioned fish stands like this one sell herring sandwiches and other fishy treats. Herring thrive in the shallow North Sea waters surrounding the Netherlands, and they're a delicacy here. While it seems the Dutch eat herring "raw," the fish is actually cured in salt (soaked for five days in an oak cask filled with a mild brine solution). Herring is caught fresh during the May/June fishing season and immediately preserved. Before the days of deep freezing, this curing process was a big deal. But these days, even Dutch herring connoisseurs admit that they can't tell what's fresh or frozen—and you get great herring all year.

Step up to the shop and see what's on ice. While herring is the star, you'll also see *garnalen* (little shrimp), *zalm* (salmon), *makreel* (mackerel), *paling* (eel), and *krabsalade* (crab salad). Most are available as a *broodje*. And every Dutch kid's favorite is *kibbeling* (deep-fried breaded cod) with a tasty sauce.

When ordering herring, you have choices. The easiest and most practical for novices is the sandwich (**broodje,** tucked into a soft roll with pickles and raw onions), while purists prefer their herring unadulterated. If you go with straight herring, your big decision is **Rotterdam-style** (pick it up by the tail, dredge it in chopped raw onions, and lower it into your mouth, all in one go) or **Amsterdam-style** (cut up in toothpick-friendly hunks, also with onions). Between the fish and the onion, herring ought to come with breath mints.

▶ *Lick your fingers—it's time to finish our walk.*

From Koningsplein you have several options. The noisy and congested Leidsestraat leads straight to the museum zone; for a more pleasant walk to the museums, follow Leidsestraat just across the next canal (Herengracht), then go left along the canal and take the first right at Nieuwe Spiegelstraat. This long street, much of it lined with art galleries and inviting shops, leads directly to the Rijksmuseum (you'll see the grand museum in the distance). Or, from near Koningsplein, you could catch tram #2 or #12 either to the museums or back to Centraal station.

But we'll finish off by following the Singel canal back to Spui Square.

⑮ From Koningsplein to Spui

With your back to the flower market, walk along the canal (with the water on your left). Follow the tram tracks as they bend around to the right and lead you to Spui.

As you walk, consider that the Singel is wide today because it was the moat and wall of the city back in the Middle Ages. In about 1620, during the golden age period of building and expansion, the wall was torn down and the city expanded with the new town across the canal to your left.

There are so many canals in Amsterdam because the city was founded in a marshy river delta, so they needed to keep the water at bay. They dammed the Amstel River and channeled it safely away into canals, creating pockets of dry land to build on.

The word *gracht* (pronounced, roughly, "hroht," with guttural flair) can refer to a canal itself, or to the ensemble of a canal and the lanes that border it. Today, the city has about 100 canals, most of which are about 10 feet deep. They're crossed by some 1,200 bridges, fringed with 100,000 Dutch elm and lime trees, and bedecked with 2,500 houseboats. A system of locks (near Centraal station) controls the flow and are opened periodically to flush out the system.

The canalside street you're enjoying was, until recently, congested with cars. Today the lanes are for bikes, trams, and people. In a few years there'll be no more fossil fuel-powered traffic in the city—the trams are already electric, all the boats will be electric...and bikes will rule.

And notice, for a minute, the bikes. For the Dutch, biking is taken very seriously. They may not wear helmets, yet they place great importance on road safety: Bikes are considered equal to cars and must follow the same rules. Stiff fines are given to those biking in pedestrian zones or looking at their phones while pedaling. Little Dutch kids grow up on bikes. At about age 10, they take a biking exam. When a fifth grader passes this exam, it's like a coming of age...their world just got bigger and more real. (The most dangerous thing on an Amsterdam road is a tourist on a bike.)

When you finally get back to **Spui,** listen to the sounds of the city: people talking over drinks at the café, bike gears changing, the *brrring* of the bells, the chatter of the birds. Does the square seem spacious? Rather than 200 cars, within view are 200 bikes. At least for the Dutch, this is the urban environment of the future.

▶ *Our walk is over. But those with more energy can consider heading to Vondelpark or the Rijksmuseum. To return to Centraal station (or to nearly any place along this walk), catch tram #2 or #12.*

Rijksmuseum Tour

At Amsterdam's Rijksmuseum ("Rijks" rhymes with "bikes"), Holland's golden age shines with the best collection anywhere of the Dutch Masters—from Vermeer's quiet domestic scenes and Steen's raucous family meals to Hals' snapshot portraits and Rembrandt's moody brilliance.

The 17th century saw the Netherlands at the pinnacle of its power. Trade and shipping boomed, wealth poured in, the people were understandably proud, and the arts flourished. Upper-middle-class businessmen hired artists to paint their portraits and decorate their homes with pretty still lifes and unpreachy, slice-of-life art.

Dutch art is meant to be enjoyed, not studied. It's straightforward, meat-and-potatoes art for the common people. On this visit, we'll enjoy the beauty of mundane things painted realistically and with exquisite detail. So set your cerebral cortex on "low" and let this art pass straight from the eyes to the heart, with minimal detours.

ORIENTATION

Cost: €22.50 timed-entry ticket, free for kids under 18.

Hours: Daily 9:00-17:00.

Information: Info tel. +31 20 674 7047, www.rijksmuseum.nl.

Advance Tickets Recommended: Purchase timed-entry tickets online in advance at www.rijksmuseum.nl. You must book an entry time even with a museum pass. Although limited walk-up tickets may be available, I recommend buying ahead.

Avoiding Crowds/Lines: Even with timed tickets, the museum is always crowded. Plan your visit for either first thing in the morning or later in the day.

Getting There: From Centraal station, catch tram #2 or #12 to the Museumplein stop. The museum entrance is inside the arched passage that cuts under the building at its center.

Tours: The museum's free app offers tours, maps, and useful info. A multimedia guide (€5) provides a 45-minute highlights tour and an in-depth version. Guided tours are available on weekends—book at least a month in advance (€5).

Length of This Tour: Allow 1.5 hours.

Baggage Check: Leave your bag at the free checkroom in the Atrium.

Cuisine Art: The Rijksmuseum Café is in the Atrium. Nearby on Museumplein, you'll find the Cobra Café and several take-out stands. Museumplein and nearby Vondelpark are both perfect for a picnic.

Starring: Rembrandt van Rijn, Frans Hals, Johannes Vermeer, Jan Steen.

The Rijksmuseum, on pleasant Museumplein

The Atrium has tourist services.

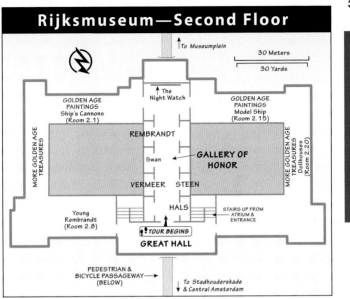

Rijksmuseum—Second Floor

To Museumplein

30 Meters
30 Yards

The Night Watch

GOLDEN AGE PAINTINGS
Ship's Cannons
(Room 2.1)

GOLDEN AGE PAINTINGS
Model Ship
(Room 2.15)

MORE GOLDEN AGE TREASURES

REMBRANDT

GALLERY OF HONOR

Swan

MORE GOLDEN AGE TREASURES
Dollhouses
(Room 2.20)

VERMEER   STEEN

HALS

STAIRS UP FROM ATRIUM & ENTRANCE

Young Rembrandt
(Room 2.8)

TOUR BEGINS

GREAT HALL

PEDESTRIAN & BICYCLE PASSAGEWAY→
(BELOW)

To Stadhouderskade
& Central Amsterdam

THE TOUR BEGINS

▶ *Descend into the lower-level Atrium. After showing your ticket (and perhaps downloading the museum app or renting a multimedia guide), follow the crowds up the stairway to the top (second) floor, where you emerge into the...*

Great Hall

With its stained-glass windows depicting great artists and thinkers, vaulted ceiling, and murals of golden age explorers, it feels like a cathedral to Holland's middle-class merchants. Gaze down the long adjoining hall to the far end, with the "altarpiece" of this cathedral—Rembrandt's *The Night Watch.*

▶ *Now, follow the flow of the crowds toward it, into the...*

Gallery of Honor

This grand space was purpose-built to hold the Greatest Hits of the golden age by the era's biggest rock stars: Hals, Vermeer, Steen, and Rembrandt. The best of the era's portraits, still lifes, landscapes, and slice-of-life "genre scenes" give us a close-up look at daily life in this happy, affluent era.

▶ *In the first alcove to the right is the work of...*

Frans Hals

Frans Hals (c. 1582-1666) was the premier golden age portrait painter. Merchants hired him the way we'd hire a wedding photographer. With a few quick strokes, Hals captured not only the features, but also the personality.

A Militiaman Holding a Berkemeyer, a.k.a. *The Merry Drinker,* c. 1628-1630

You're greeted by a jovial man in a black hat, capturing the earthy, exuberant spirit of the Dutch golden age. Notice the details—the happy red face of the man offering us a *berkemeyer* drinking glass, the sparkle in his eyes, the lacy collar, the decorative belt buckle, and so on.

Now move in closer. All these meticulous details are accomplished with a few thick, messy brushstrokes. The beard is a tangle of brown worms, the belt buckle a yellow blur. His hand is a study in smudges. Even the expressive face is created with a few well-chosen patches of color. Unlike Dutch still-life scenes, this canvas is meant to be viewed from a distance, where the colors and brushstrokes blend together.

Rather than posing his subjects, making them stand for hours saying "cheese," Hals tried to catch them at a candid moment. He often painted common people, fishermen, and barflies such as this one. He had to work quickly to capture the serendipity of the moment. Hals used a stop-action technique, freezing the man in mid-gesture, with the rough brushwork creating a blur that suggests the man is still moving.

Two centuries later, the Impressionists learned from Hals' scruffy brushwork. In the Van Gogh Museum, you'll see how Van Gogh painted, say, a brown beard by using thick dabs of green, yellow, and red that blend at a distance to make brown.

The Dutch Golden Age (1600s)

Who bought this art? Look around at the Rijksmuseum's many portraits and you'll see ordinary middle-class people, merchants, and traders. Even in their Sunday best, you can tell that these are hardworking, businesslike, friendly, simple people (with a penchant for ruffled lace collars).

By 1600, Holland's merchant fleets ruled the waves with colonies as far away as India, the East Indies, and America (remember—New York was originally "New Amsterdam"). Back home, these traders were financed by shrewd Amsterdam businessmen on the new frontiers of capitalism.

Look around again. Is there even one crucifixion? One saint? One Madonna? In most countries, Catholic bishops and rich kings supported the arts. But the Dutch Republic was independent, democratic, and largely Protestant, with no taste for saints and Madonnas.

Instead, Dutch burghers bought portraits of themselves and pretty, unpreachy, unpretentious works for their homes—landscapes, portraits (often of groups), scenes from everyday life, and still lifes of food and mundane objects.

Portrait of a Couple, Probably Isaac Abrahamsz Massa and Beatrix van der Laen, c. 1622

This likely wedding portrait of a chubby, pleasant merchant and his bride sums up the story of the Dutch golden age. Because this overseas trader was away from home for years at a time on business, Hals makes a special effort to point out his patron's commitment to marriage. Isaac pledges allegiance to his wife, putting his hand on his heart. Beatrix's wedding ring is prominently displayed dead center between them (on her right-hand forefinger, Protestant-style). The vine clinging to a tree is a symbol of man's support and woman's dependence. And in the distance at right, in the classical love garden, are other happy couples strolling arm-in-arm amid peacocks, a symbol of fertility.

In earlier times, marriage portraits put the man and wife in separate canvases, staring out grimly. Hals' jolly side-by-side couple reflects a societal shift from marriage as business partnership to an arrangement that's more friendly and intimate.

Hals didn't need symbolism to tell us that these two are prepared for their long-distance relationship—they seem relaxed together, but each looks at us directly, with a strong, individual identity. Good as gold, these are the type of people who propelled this soggy little country into its glorious golden age.

▶ *A little farther along are the small-scale canvases of...*

Johannes Vermeer

Vermeer (1632-1675) is the master of tranquility and stillness. He creates a clear and silent pool that is a world in itself. Most of his canvases show interiors of Dutch homes, where Dutch women engage in everyday activities, lit by a side window.

Vermeer's father, an art dealer, gave Johannes a passion for painting. Late in the artist's career, with Holland drained by wars against England, the demand for art and luxuries went sour, forcing Vermeer to downsize—he sold his big home, packed up his wife and 14 children, and moved in with his mother-in-law. He died two years later, and his works fell into centuries of obscurity.

The Rijksmuseum has the best collection of Vermeers in the world—four of them. (There are only some 34 in captivity.) But each is a small jewel worth lingering over.

The Milkmaid, c. 1660

It's so quiet you can practically hear the milk pouring into the bowl.

Vermeer brings out the beauty in everyday things. The subject is ordinary—a kitchen maid—but you could look for hours at the tiny details and rich color tones. These are everyday objects, but they glow in a diffused light: the crunchy crust, the hanging basket, even the rusty nail in the wall with its tiny shadow. Vermeer had a unique ability with surface texture, to show how things feel when you touch them.

The maid is alive with Vermeer's distinctive yellow and blue—the colors of many traditional Dutch homes—against a white backdrop. She is content, solid, and sturdy, performing this simple task as if it's

Vermeer's *Milkmaid*—quiet beauty

Woman Reading a Letter—from whom?

the most important thing in the world. Her full arms are built with patches of reflected light. Vermeer squares off a little world in itself (framed by the table in the foreground, the wall in back, the window to the left, and the footstool at right), then fills this space with objects for our perusal.

Woman Reading a Letter, c. 1663
Notice how Vermeer's placid scenes often have an air of mystery. The woman is reading a letter. From whom? A lover? A father on a two-year business trip to the East Indies? Not even taking time to sit down, she reads intently, with parted lips and a bowed head. It must be important. (She looks pregnant, adding to the mystery, but that may just be the cut of her clothes.)

Again, Vermeer has framed a moment of everyday life. But within this small world are hints of a wider, wilder world—the light coming from the left is obviously from a large window, giving us a whiff of the life going on outside. The map hangs prominently, reminding us of travel, and perhaps of where the letter is from.

The Love Letter, c. 1669-1670
There's a similar theme here. The curtain parts, and we see through the doorway into a dollhouse world, then through the seascape on the back wall to the wide ocean. A woman is playing a lute when she's interrupted by a servant bringing a letter. The mysterious letter stops the music, intruding like a pebble dropped into the pool of Vermeer's quiet world. The floor tiles create a strong 3-D perspective that sucks us straight into the center of the painting—the woman's heart.

Vermeer's *The Love Letter*

View of Houses in Delft—Vermeer's hometown

View of Houses in Delft, a.k.a. *The Little Street*, c. 1658

Vermeer was born in the picturesque town of Delft, grew up near its Market Square, and set a number of his paintings there. This may be the view from his front door.

The details in the painting actually aren't very detailed—the cobblestone street doesn't have a single individual stone in it. But Vermeer shows us the beautiful interplay of colored rectangles on the buildings. Our eye moves back and forth from shutter to gable to window...and then from front to back, as we notice the woman deep in the alleyway.

▶ *In an alcove nearby are some rollicking paintings by...*

Jan Steen

Not everyone could afford a masterpiece, but even poorer people wanted works of art for their homes (like a landscape from Sears for over the sofa). Jan Steen (c. 1625-1679, pronounced "yahn stain"), the Norman Rockwell of his day, painted humorous scenes from the lives of the lower classes. As a tavern owner, he observed society firsthand.

The Feast of St. Nicholas, 1665-1668

It's Christmas time, and the kids have been given their gifts, including a little girl who got a doll. The mother says, "Let me see it," but the girl turns away playfully. Everyone is happy except the boy, who's crying. His Christmas present is only a branch in his shoe—like coal in your stocking, the gift for bad boys. His sister gloats and passes it around. The kids laugh at him. But wait—it turns out the family is just playing a trick. In the background, the grandmother beckons to him, saying, "Look, I have your real present in here." Out of the limelight,

Shhh...Dutch Art

You're sitting at home late one night, and it's perfectly calm. Not a sound, very peaceful. And then...the refrigerator motor turns off, and it's really quiet.

Dutch art is really quiet art. It silences our busy world, so that every sound, every motion is noticeable. You can hear cows tearing off grass 50 yards away. We notice how the cold night air makes the stars sharp.

One of the museum's most exciting, dramatic, emotional, and extravagant Dutch paintings is probably *The Threatened Swan* (in the Gallery of Honor). It's quite a contrast to the rape scenes and visions of heaven of Italian Baroque paintings from the same time period.

but smack in the middle, sits the father providing ballast to this family scene and clearly enjoying his children's pleasure.

Steen has frozen the moment, sliced off a piece, and laid it on a canvas. He's told a story with a past, a present, and a future. These are real people in a real scene.

Steen's fun art reminds us that museums aren't mausoleums.

Adolf and Catharina Croeser, a.k.a. The Burgomaster of Delft and His Daughter, 1655

Steen's well-dressed burgher sits on his front porch, when a poor woman and child approach to beg, putting him squarely between the horns of a moral dilemma. On the one hand, we see his rich home, well-dressed daughter, and a vase of flowers—a symbol that his money came from morally suspect capitalism (the kind that produced the folly of 1637's "tulip mania"). On the other hand, there are his poor

Steen—playful family scene at Christmas   Steen—a rich burgher's moral dilemma

fellow citizens and the church steeple, reminding him of his Christian duty. The man's daughter avoids the confrontation. Will the burgher set the right Christian example? This moral dilemma perplexed many nouveau-riche Dutch Calvinists of Steen's day.

This early painting by Steen demonstrates his mastery of several popular genres: portrait, still life (the flowers and fabrics), cityscape, and moral instruction.

The Merry Family, 1668

This family—three generations living happily under one roof—is eating, drinking, and singing like there's no tomorrow. The broken eggshells and scattered cookware symbolize waste and extravagance. The neglected proverb tacked to the fireplace reminds us that children will follow in the footsteps of their parents. The father in this jolly scene is very drunk—ready to topple over—while in the foreground his mischievous daughter is feeding her brother wine straight from the flask. Mom and Grandma join the artist himself (playing the bagpipes)

Steen's *Merry Family* may not be morally upright, but they sure know how to have fun.

in a lively sing-along, but the child learning to smoke would rather follow Dad's lead.

Dutch golden age families were notoriously lenient with their kids. Even today, the Dutch describe a rowdy family as a "Jan Steen household."

▶ *You're getting closer to the iconic* Night Watch, *but first you'll find other works by…*

Rembrandt van Rijn

Rembrandt van Rijn (1606-1669) is the greatest of all Dutch painters. Whereas most painters specialized in one field—portraits, landscapes, still lifes—Rembrandt excelled in them all.

The son of a Leiden miller who owned a waterwheel on the Rhine ("van Rijn"), Rembrandt took Amsterdam by storm with his famous painting *The Anatomy Lesson of Dr. Nicolaes Tulp* (1632, currently in The Hague). The commissions poured in for official portraits, and he was soon wealthy and married (1634) to Saskia van Uylenburgh. They moved to an expensive home in the Jewish Quarter (today's Rembrandt House Museum) and decorated it with their collection of art and exotic furniture. His portraits were dutifully detailed, but other paintings explored strong contrasts of light and dark, with dramatic composition.

In 1642, Saskia died, and Rembrandt's fortunes changed, as the public's taste shifted and commissions dried up. In 1649, he hired an 18-year-old model named Hendrickje Stoffels, and she soon moved in with him and gave birth to their daughter.

Holland's war with England (1652-1654) devastated the art market, and Rembrandt's free-spending ways forced him to declare bankruptcy (1656)—the ultimate humiliation in success-oriented Amsterdam. The commissions came more slowly. The money ran out. His mother died. He had to auction off his paintings and furniture to pay debts. He moved out of his fine house to a cheaper place on Rozengracht. His bitter losses added a new wisdom to his work.

In his last years, Rembrandt's greatest works were his self-portraits, showing a tired, wrinkled man stoically enduring life's misfortunes. Rembrandt piled on layers of paint and glaze to capture increasingly subtle effects. In 1668, his lone surviving son, Titus, died, and

Ruffs

I cannot tell you why men and women of the Dutch golden age found these fanlike collars attractive, but they certainly were all the rage here and elsewhere in Europe. It started in Spain in the 1540s, but the style really took off with a marvelous discovery in 1565: starch. Within decades, Europe's wealthy merchant class was wearing nine-inch collars made from 18 yards of material.

The ruffs were detachable and made from a long, pleated strip of linen set into a neck (or wrist) band. You tied it in front with strings. Big ones required that you wear a wire frame underneath for support. There were various types—the "cartwheel" was the biggest, a "double ruff" had two layers of pleats, and a "cabbage" was somewhat asymmetrical.

Ruffs required elaborate maintenance. First, you washed and starched the linen. While the cloth was still wet, hot metal pokers were painstakingly inserted into the folds to form the characteristic figure-eight pattern. The ruffs were stored in special round boxes to hold their shape.

For about a century, Europeans loved the ruff, but by 1630, Holland had come to its senses, and the fad faded.

Rembrandt passed away the next year. His death effectively marked the end of the Dutch golden age.

Isaac and Rebecca, a.k.a. The Jewish Bride, c. 1665-1669

The man gently draws the woman toward him. She's comfortable enough with him to sink into thought, and she reaches up unconsciously to return the gentle touch. They're young but wizened. This uncommissioned portrait (its subjects remain unknown) is a truly human look at the relationship between two people in love. They form a protective pyramid of love amid a gloomy background. The touching hands form the center of this somewhat sad but peaceful work. Van

Gogh said that "Rembrandt alone has that tenderness—the heartbroken tenderness."

Rembrandt was a master of oil painting. In his later years, he rendered details with a messier, more Impressionistic style. The red-brown-gold of the couple's clothes is a patchwork of oil laid on thick with a palette knife.

The Wardens of the Amsterdam Drapers Guild, a.k.a. *The Syndics,* 1662

Rembrandt could paint an official group portrait better than anyone. In the painting made famous by Dutch Masters cigars, he catches the Drapers Guild in a natural but dignified pose (dignified, at least, until the guy on the left sits on his friend's lap).

It's a business meeting, and they're all dressed in black with black hats—the standard power suit of the Dutch golden age. They gather around a table examining the company's books. Suddenly, someone (us) walks in, and they look up. It's as natural as a snapshot, though X-rays show Rembrandt made many changes in posing them perfectly.

The figures are "framed" by the table beneath them and the top of the wood paneling above their heads, making a three-part composition that brings this band of colleagues together. Even in this simple portrait, we feel we can read the guild members' personalities in their faces. (If the table in the painting looks like it's sloping a bit unnaturally, lie on the floor to view it at Rembrandt's intended angle.)

▶ *At the far end of the Gallery of Honor is the museum's star masterpiece. The best viewing spot is to the right of center—the angle Rembrandt had in mind when he designed it.*

Rembrandt's tender *Jewish Bride*

Drapers Guild—meeting interrupted

The Night Watch, a.k.a. The Militia Company of Captain Frans Banninck Cocq, 1642

This is Rembrandt's most famous—though not necessarily greatest—painting. It's displayed behind glass and is being carefully studied by conservators as they determine the best way to combat deterioration.

Created in 1642, when Rembrandt was 36, *The Night Watch* was one of his most important commissions: a group portrait of a company of Amsterdam's Civic Guards to hang in their meeting hall.

It's an action shot. With flags waving and drums beating, the guardsmen (who, by the 1640s, were really only an honorary militia of rich bigwigs) spill onto the street from under an arch in the back. It's "all for one and one for all" as they rush to Amsterdam's rescue. The soldiers grab lances and load their muskets. In the center, the commander (in black, with a red sash) strides forward energetically with a hand gesture that seems to say, "What are we waiting for? Let's move out!" His lieutenant focuses on his every order.

Rembrandt caught the optimistic spirit of Holland in the 1600s. Its war of independence from Spain was heading to victory and the economy was booming. These guardsmen on the move epitomize the proud, independent, upwardly mobile Dutch.

Why is *The Night Watch* so famous? Compare it with other, less famous group portraits nearby, where every face is visible and everyone

Rembrandt's famous *Night Watch*—Civic Guards in action

is well-lit, flat, and flashbulb-perfect. These people paid good money to have their mugs preserved for posterity, and they wanted it right up front. Other group portraits may be colorful, dignified works by a master...but not quite masterpieces.

By contrast, Rembrandt rousted the Civic Guards off their fat duffs. By adding movement and depth to an otherwise static scene, he took posers and turned them into warriors. He turned a simple portrait into great art.

OK, some *Night Watch* scuttlebutt: First off, "night watch" is a misnomer. It's a daytime scene, but over the years, as the preserving varnish darkened and layers of dirt built up, the sun set on this painting, and it got its popular title. When the painting was moved to a smaller room, the sides were lopped off (and the pieces lost), putting the two main characters in the center and causing the work to become more static than intended. During World War II, the painting was rolled up and hidden for five years. In 1975, a madman attacked the painting, slicing the captain's legs, and in 1990, it was sprayed with acid (it was skillfully restored after both incidents).

The Night Watch, contrary to popular myth, was a smashing success in its day. However, there are elements in it that show why Rembrandt fell out of favor as a portrait painter. He seemed to spend as much time painting the dwarf and the mysterious glowing girl with a chicken (the very appropriate mascot of this "militia" of shopkeepers) as he did the faces of his employers.

Rembrandt's life darkened long before his *Night Watch* did. This work marks the peak of Rembrandt's popularity...and the beginning of his fall from grace. He continued to paint masterpieces. Free from the dictates of employers whose taste was in their mouths, he painted what he wanted, how he wanted it. Rembrandt goes beyond mere craftsmanship to probe into, and draw life from, the deepest wells of the human soul.

▶ *Backtrack a few steps to the Gallery of Honor's last alcove to find Rembrandt's...*

Self-Portrait as the Apostle Paul, 1661

Rembrandt's many self-portraits show us the evolution of a great painter's style, as well as the progress of a genius's life. For Rembrandt, the two were intertwined.

In this somber, late self-portrait, the man is 55 but he looks 70.

With a lined forehead, a bulbous nose, and messy hair, he peers out from under several coats of glazing, holding old, wrinkled pages. His look is...skeptical? Weary? Resigned to life's misfortunes? Or amused? (He's looking at us, but not *just* at us—remember that a self-portrait is done staring into a mirror.)

This man has seen it all—success, love, money, fatherhood, loss, poverty, death. He took these experiences and wove them into his art. Rembrandt died poor and misunderstood, but he remained very much his own man to the end.

▶ *You'll find more Rembrandts in Room 2.8, located a half-dozen rooms to the left of* The Night Watch.

Self-Portrait, c. 1628

Here we see the young small-town boy about to launch himself into whatever life has to offer. Rembrandt was a precocious kid. His father, a miller, insisted that he become a lawyer. His mother hoped he'd be a preacher (you may see a portrait of her reading the Bible). Rembrandt combined the secular and religious worlds by becoming an artist, someone who can hint at the spiritual by showing us the beauty of the created world.

He moved to Amsterdam and entered the highly competitive art world. Amsterdam was a booming town and, like today, a hip and cosmopolitan city. Rembrandt portrays himself at age 22 as being divided—half in light, half hidden by hair and shadows—open-eyed, but wary of an uncertain future. Rembrandt's paintings are often light and dark, both in color and in subject, exploring the "darker" side of human experience.

Self-Portrait: These eyes have seen it all.

Young Rembrandt—what does his future hold?

Portrait of a Woman, Possibly Maria Trip, 1639

This debutante daughter of a wealthy citizen is shy and reserved—maybe a bit awkward in her new dress and adult role, but still self-assured. When he chose to, Rembrandt could dash off a commissioned portrait like nobody's business. The details are immaculate—the lace and shiny satin, the pearls behind the veil, the subtle face and hands. Rembrandt gives us not just a person, but a personality.

Look at the red rings around her eyes, a detail a lesser painter would have airbrushed out. Rembrandt takes this feature, unique to her, and uses it as a setting for her luminous, jewel-like eyes. Without being prettified, she's beautiful.

Young Woman in Fantasy Costume, Possibly Saskia, 1633

It didn't take long for Amsterdam to recognize Rembrandt's great talent. Everyone wanted a portrait done by the young master, and he became wealthy and famous. He fell in love with and married the rich, beautiful, and cultured Saskia. By all accounts, the two were enormously happy, entertaining friends, decorating their house with fine furniture, raising a family, and living the high life. In this painting, Saskia's face literally glows, and a dash of white paint puts a sparkle in her eye. Barely 30 years old, Rembrandt was the most successful painter in Holland. He had it all.

Jeremiah Lamenting the Destruction of Jerusalem, 1630

The Babylonians have sacked and burned Jerusalem, but Rembrandt leaves the pyrotechnics (in the murky background at left) to Spielberg and the big screen. Instead, he tells the story of Israel's destruction in the face of the prophet who predicted the disaster. Jeremiah slumps in defeat, deep in thought, confused and despondent, trying to

Maria Trip radiates honest beauty.

Jeremiah—brooding in the darkness

understand why this evil had to happen. Rembrandt turns his flood-light of truth on the prophet's deeply lined forehead.

Rembrandt wasn't satisfied to crank out portraits of fat merchants in frilly bibs, no matter what they paid him. He wanted to experiment, trying new techniques and more probing subjects. Many of his paintings weren't commissioned and were never even intended for sale. His subjects could be brooding and melancholy, a bit dark for the public's taste. His technique set him apart—you can recognize a Rembrandt canvas by his play of light and dark. Most of his paintings are a deep brown tone, with only a few bright spots glowing from the darkness. This allowed Rembrandt to highlight the details he thought most important and to express moody emotions.

▶ *Finish your tour with another painting here in Room 2.8. It's a large group portrait by Bartholomeus van der Helst, called...*

The Banquet at the Crossbowmen's Guild, 1648

This colorful portrait of several dozen Amsterdammers was painted to celebrate Holland's new era of peace after its war with Spain. Though shown in military uniforms, these men were really captains of industry—shipbuilders, seamen, salesmen, spice tasters, bankers, and venture capitalists. This group portrait captures the prosperity and can-do spirit of the Dutch golden age.

The Rest of the Rijks

The museum is most famous for the paintings you've just seen. But with a collection of 8,000 works—detailing Dutch history from 1200 to the present—the Rijks offers much, much more.

Bartholomeus Van der Helst's glorious group portrait is just one of many golden age treasures.

Level 2: The second floor is home to more golden age artifacts. Keep circling the floor counterclockwise, keeping an eye out for a stunning collection of blue-and-white Delftware, dollhouses, and a big wooden model of a 74-gun Dutch man-of-war.

Level 1: There's a Van Gogh self-portrait that portrays him with the bright, thick brushstrokes that would become his signature.

Level 0: This has everything from women's fashion to more Delftware. The Asian Art Pavilion shows off objects from the East Indies—a former Dutch colony—as well as items from India, Japan, Korea, and China.

Level 3: Finally, you could ride the elevator up to the top floor for exhibits from the 20th century, including an airplane, bringing you right up to the present.

Van Gogh Museum Tour

The Van Gogh Museum (we say "van GO," the Dutch say "van hock") is a cultural high even for those not into art. Located near the Rijksmuseum, the museum houses the 200 paintings owned by Vincent's younger brother, Theo. It's a user-friendly stroll through the work and life of one enigmatic man. If you like brightly colored landscapes in the Impressionist style, you'll like this museum. If you enjoy finding deeper meaning in works of art, you'll really love it. The mix of Van Gogh's creative genius, his tumultuous life, and the traveler's perspective makes this museum as much a walk with Vincent as with his art.

Cost: €20 timed-entry ticket, not covered by I Amsterdam City Card.

Hours: Daily 9:00-17:00, may stay open later in summer, shorter hours off-season.

Information: +31 20 570 5200, www.vangoghmuseum.com.

Advance Tickets Required: To assure you'll get in (and avoid a wait), buy timed-entry tickets at least a week in advance at www.vangoghmuseum.com. Even with a museum pass, you must reserve a time slot in advance. Same-day tickets are usually unavailable.

When to Go: To avoid crowds, aim for the earliest entry time slot you can. Midmornings are the most crowded.

Getting There: It's the big, modern, gray-and-beige place on Museumplein. From Centraal station, catch tram #2 or #12 to the Museumplein stop.

Getting In: Pass through security into the glass-pavilion entrance hall. Here you'll find an info desk, bag check, multimedia-guide rental, and WCs. There's also a gift shop (a second, less-crowded gift shop is on level 0). Don't overlook the doorway leading to an excellent temporary exhibit gallery (generally free).

Tours: The 45-minute multimedia guide (€3.50) provides insightful commentary on Van Gogh's paintings and his technique, along with related quotes from Vincent himself.

Length of This Tour: Allow one hour.

Baggage Check: Free and mandatory.

Cuisine Art: The museum has a cafeteria-style café on level 0 and a coffee/pastry stand in the entrance hall.

The Van Gogh Museum on Museumplein

Avoid crowds by visiting on Friday evening.

THE TOUR BEGINS

The collection is laid out roughly chronologically, tracing the changes in Vincent van Gogh's life and styles. You'll start on level 0, where self-portraits introduce you to the artist. Level 1 has his early paintings, level 2 focuses on the man and his contemporaries, and level 3 has his final works. But be flexible: Curators move the paintings around to illustrate various themes.

▶ *From the entrance hall, make your way up an escalator to the permanent collection, arriving on **level 0**.*

Vincent van Gogh, 1853–1890
I am a man of passions...

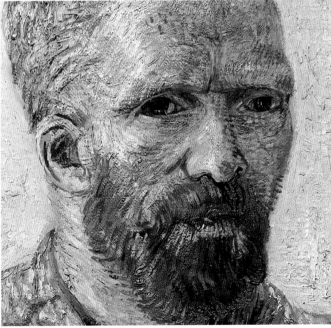

Self-portraits capture Vincent at various stages of his short life.

You could see Vincent van Gogh's canvases as a series of suicide notes—or as the record of a life full of beauty...perhaps too full of beauty. He attacked life with a passion, experiencing highs and lows more intensely than the average person. The beauty of the world overwhelmed him; its ugliness struck him as only another dimension of beauty. He tried to absorb the full spectrum of experience, good and bad, and channel it onto a canvas. The frustration of this overwhelming task drove him to madness. If all this is a bit overstated—and I guess it is—it's an attempt to show the emotional impact that Van Gogh's works have had on many people, me included.

Vincent, a pastor's son from a small Dutch town, started working at age 16 as a clerk for an art dealer. But his two interests, art and religion, distracted him from his dreary work, and after several years, he was fired.

The next 10 years were a collage of dead ends as he traveled northern Europe pursuing one path after another. He launched into each project with incredible energy, then became disillusioned and moved on to something else: teacher at a boarding school, assistant preacher, bookstore apprentice, preacher again, theology student, English student, literature student, art student. He bounced around England, France, Belgium, and the Netherlands. He fell in love but was rejected for someone more respectable. He quarreled with his family and was estranged. He lived with a prostitute and her daughter, offending the few friends he had. Finally, in his late 20s, worn out, flat broke, and in poor health, he returned to his family in Nuenen and made peace. He then started to paint.

▶ *Ascend to* **level 1.** *Work clockwise around the floor and follow the stages of Vincent's life. Start with his stark, dark early work.*

The Netherlands, 1880-1885

Peasants, Poverty, and Religion

These dark, gray-brown canvases show us the hard, plain existence of the people and town of Nuenen in the rural southern Netherlands. Van Gogh painted the town's simple buildings, bare or autumnal trees, and overcast skies—a world where it seems spring will never arrive. What warmth there is comes from the sturdy, gentle people themselves.

The style is crude—Van Gogh couldn't draw very well and would never become a great technician. The paint is laid on thick, as though painted with Nuenen mud. The main subject is almost always dead center, with little or no background, so there's a claustrophobic feeling. We are unable to see anything but the immediate surroundings.

The Potato Eaters, 1885

Those that prefer to see the peasants in their Sunday-best may do as they like. I personally am convinced I get better results by painting them in their roughness... If a peasant picture smells of bacon, smoke, potato steam—all right, that's healthy.

In a dark, cramped room lit only by a dim lamp, poor workers help themselves to a steaming plate of potatoes. They've earned it. Vincent deliberately wanted the canvas to be potato-colored.

He had dabbled as an artist during his wandering years, sketching things around him and taking a few art classes, but it wasn't until age 29 that Vincent painted his first oil canvas. He soon threw himself into it with abandon.

He painted the poor working peasants. He knew them well, having worked as a lay minister among peasants and miners. He joined them at work in the mines, taught their children, and even gave away his few possessions to help them. The church authorities finally dismissed him for "excessive zeal," but he came away understanding the poor's harsh existence and the dignity with which they bore it.

Still Life with Bible, 1885

I have a terrible need of—shall I say the word?—religion. Then I go out and paint the stars.

The Bible and Émile Zola's *La Joie de Vivre*—these two books dominated Van Gogh's life. In his art he tried to fuse his religious upbringing with his love of the world's beauty. He lusted after life with a religious

Potato Eaters—the peasants he worked with

Still Life with Bible—son of a minister

fervor. The burned-out candle tells us of the recent death of his father. The Bible is open to Isaiah 53: "He was despised and rejected of men, a man of sorrows..."

The Old Church Tower at Nuenen, a.k.a. The Peasants' Churchyard, 1885

The crows circle above the local cemetery of Nuenen. Soon after his father's death, Vincent—in poor health and depressed—moved briefly to Antwerp. He then decided to visit his younger brother Theo, an art dealer living in Paris, the art capital of the world. Theo's support—financial and emotional—allowed Vincent to spend the rest of his short life painting.

Vincent moved from rural, religious, poor Holland to Paris, the City of Light. Vincent van Gone.

▶ *Continue to the room with work he did in...*

Paris, March 1886-February 1888

Impressionism

The sun begins to break through, lighting up everything he paints. His canvases are more colorful and the landscapes more spacious, with plenty of open sky, giving a feeling of exhilaration after the closed, dark world of Nuenen.

In the cafés and bars of Paris' bohemian Montmartre district, Vincent met the revolutionary Impressionists. He roomed with Theo and became friends with other struggling young painters, such as Paul Gauguin and Henri de Toulouse-Lautrec. His health improved. He became more sociable, had an affair with an older woman, and was generally happy.

Gloomy church tower in hometown Nuenen

In Paris, the artist found bright colors.

He signed up to study under a well-known classical teacher but quit after only a few classes. He couldn't afford to hire models, so he roamed the streets, sketch pad in hand, and learned from his Impressionist friends.

The Impressionists emphasized getting out of the stuffy studio and setting up canvases outside on the street or in the countryside to paint the play of sunlight off the trees, buildings, and water.

As you see in this room, at first, Vincent copied from the Impressionist masters. He painted garden scenes like Claude Monet, café snapshots like Edgar Degas, "block prints" like the Japanese masters, and self-portraits like...nobody else.

Self-Portrait as a Painter, 1887-1888
I am now living with my brother Vincent, who is studying the art of painting with indefatigable zeal.
>—Theo van Gogh to a friend

Here, the budding young artist proudly displays his new palette full of bright colors, trying his hand at the Impressionist technique of building a scene using dabs of different-colored paint. A whole new world of art—and life—opened up to him in Paris.

Self-Portrait with Straw Hat, 1887
You wouldn't recognize Vincent, he has changed so much... The doctor says that he is now perfectly fit again. He is making tremendous strides with his work... He is also far livelier than he used to be and is popular with people.
>—Theo van Gogh to their mother

In Paris, Vincent learned the Impressionist painting technique. The shimmering effect comes from placing dabs of different colors side by

With straw hat and pipe, he painted outdoors.   Traditional still life with modern colors

side on the canvas. At a distance, the two colors blend in the eye of the viewer to become a single color. Here, Vincent uses separate strokes of blue, yellow, green, and red to create a brown beard—but a brown that throbs with excitement.

Red Cabbages and Onions, 1887

Vincent quickly developed his own style: thicker paint; broad, swirling brushstrokes; and brighter, clashing colors that make even inanimate objects seem to pulsate with life. The many different colors are supposed to blend together, but you'd have to back up to Belgium to make these colors resolve into focus.

Self-Portrait with Gray Felt Hat, 1887

He has painted one or two portraits which have turned out well, but he insists on working for nothing. It is a pity that he shows no desire to earn some money because he could easily do so here. But you can't change people.
    —Theo van Gogh to their mother

Despite his new sociability, Vincent never quite fit in with his Impressionist friends. As he developed into a good painter, he became anxious to strike out on his own. He thought the social life of the big city was distracting him from serious work. In this painting, his face screams out from a swirling background of molecular activity. He wanted peace and quiet, a place where he could throw himself into his work completely. He headed for the sunny south of France.

▶ *Travel to the far end of the room, where you finally reach...*

Arles, February 1888-May 1889

Sunlight, Beauty, and Madness

Winter was just turning to spring when Vincent arrived in Arles, near the French Riviera. After the dreary Paris winter, the colors of springtime overwhelmed him. The blossoming trees and colorful fields inspired him to paint canvas after canvas, drenched in sunlight.

The Yellow House, a.k.a. The Street, 1888

It is my intention...to go temporarily to the South, where there is even more color, even more sun.

Vincent rented this house with the green shutters. (He ate at the pink café next door.) Look at that blue sky! He painted in a frenzy, working

Thick brushstrokes radiate outward, magnifying the artist's ultra-intense gaze.

feverishly to try and take it all in. For the next nine months, he produced an explosion of canvases, working very quickly when the mood possessed him. His unique style evolved beyond Impressionism—thicker paint, stronger outlines, brighter colors (often applied right from the paint tube), and swirling brushwork that makes inanimate objects pulse and vibrate with life.

The Bedroom, 1888
I am a man of passions, capable of and subject to doing more or less foolish things—which I happen to regret, more or less, afterwards.

His *Yellow House* in sunny Arles

His bedroom, fit for the monastic artist

Vincent was alone, a Dutchman in Provence. And that had its down-side. Vincent swung from flurries of ecstatic activity to bouts of great loneliness. Like anyone traveling alone, he experienced those high highs and low lows. This narrow, trapezoid-shaped, single-room apartment (less than 200 square feet) must have seemed like a prison cell at times. (Psychologists have pointed out that most everything in this painting comes in pairs—two chairs, two paintings, a double bed squeezed down to a single—indicating his desire for a mate. Hmm.)

He invited his friend Paul Gauguin to join him, envisioning a sort of artists' colony in Arles. He spent months preparing a room upstairs for Gauguin's arrival.

Sunflowers, 1889

The worse I get along with people, the more I learn to have faith in Nature and concentrate on her.

Vincent saw sunflowers as his signature subject, and he painted a half-dozen versions of them, each a study in intense yellow. If he signed the work (look on the vase), it means he was proud of it.

Even a simple work like these sunflowers bursts with life. Different people see different things in *Sunflowers*. Is it a happy painting, or is it a melancholy one? Take your own emotional temperature and see.

The Sower, 1888

A dark, silhouetted figure sows seeds in the burning sun. It's late in the day. The heat from the sun, the source of all life, radiates out in thick swirls of paint. The sower must be a hopeful man, because the field looks slanted and barren. Someday, he thinks, the seeds he's planting will grow into something great, like the tree that slashes

When Van Gogh signed a painting (like *Sunflowers*), it meant he was proud of it.

diagonally across the scene—tough and craggy, but with small, optimistic blossoms.

In his younger years, Vincent had worked in Belgium sowing the Christian gospel in a harsh environment (see Mark 4:1-9). Now in Arles, ignited by the sun, he cast his artistic seeds to the wind, hoping.

Gauguin's Chair, 1888

Empty chairs—there are many of them, there will be even more, and sooner or later, there will be nothing but empty chairs.

Gauguin arrived. At first, he and Vincent got along great. But then things went sour. They clashed over art, life, and their prickly personalities. On Christmas Eve 1888, Vincent went ballistic. Enraged during an alcohol-fueled argument, he pulled out a razor and waved it in Gauguin's face. Gauguin took the hint and quickly left town. Vincent was horrified at himself. In a fit of remorse and madness, he mutilated his own ear and presented it to a prostitute.

The people of Arles realized they had a madman on their hands. A doctor diagnosed "acute mania with hallucinations," and the local vicar talked Vincent into admitting himself to a peaceful mental hospital. Vincent wrote to Theo: "Temporarily I wish to remain shut up, as much for my own peace of mind as for other people's."

▶ *Ascend to **level 2,** which is less about Van Gogh's paintings than about his relationships with family and friends, and his artistic process. To see his final paintings, continue up to **level 3.***

St-Remy, May 1889-May 1890

The Mental Hospital

In the mental hospital, Vincent kept painting whenever he was well enough. He often couldn't go out, so he copied from books, making his own distinctive versions of works by Rembrandt, Delacroix, Millet, and others.

At first, the peace and quiet of the asylum did Vincent good, and his health improved. Occasionally, he was allowed outside to paint the gardens and landscapes. Meanwhile, the paintings he had been sending to Theo began to attract attention in Paris for the first time. A woman in Brussels bought one of his canvases—the only painting he ever sold during his lifetime. In 1987, one of his *Sunflowers* sold for $40

Gauguin's Chair: When his friend visited, Vincent drove him away in a fit of madness.

million. Three years later a portrait of Vincent's doctor went for more than $80 million.

At St-Remy, we see a change from bright, happy landscapes to more introspective subjects. The colors are less bright and more surreal, the brushwork even more furious. The strong outlines of figures are twisted and tortured.

The Garden of Saint Paul's Hospital, a.k.a. Leaf Fall, 1889

A traveler going to a destination that does not exist...

The stark brown trees are blown by the wind. A solitary figure (Vincent?) winds along a narrow, snaky path as the wind blows leaves on him. The colors are surreal—blue, green, and red tree trunks with heavy black outlines. A road runs away from us, heading nowhere.

The Sheaf Binder, After Millet, 1889

I want to paint men and women with that something of the eternal which the halo used to symbolize...

Vincent's compassion for honest laborers remained constant. These sturdy folk, with their curving bodies, wrestle as one with their curving wheat. The world Vincent sees is charged from within by spiritual fires, twisting and turning matter into energy, and vice versa.

Wheat Field with a Reaper, 1889

I have been working hard and fast in the last few days. This is how I try to express how desperately fast things pass in modern life.

The harvest is here. The time is short. There's much work to be done. A lone reaper works uphill, scything through a swirling wheat field, cutting slender paths of calm. Vincent saw the reaper—a figure of impending death—as the flip side of the sower.

Vincent portrays workers with noble dignity.

The trees ripple with an inner force.

Pietà, After Delacroix, 1889

It's evening after a thunderstorm. Jesus has been crucified, and the corpse lies at the mouth of a tomb. Mary, whipped by the cold wind, holds her empty arms out in despair and confusion. She is the tender mother who receives us all in death, as though saying, "My child, you've been away so long—rest in my arms." Christ has a Vincent-esque red beard.

Auvers-sur-Oise, May-July 1890

The bird looks through the bars at the overcast sky where a thunderstorm is gathering, and inwardly he rebels against his fate. 'I am caged, I am caged, and you tell me I have everything I need! Oh! I beg you, give me liberty, that I may be a bird like other birds.' A certain idle man resembles this idle bird...

Though Van Gogh wished to be free of the mental hospital, his fits of madness would not relent. During these spells, he lost all sense of his own actions. He couldn't paint, the one thing he felt driven to do. He wrote to Theo, "My surroundings here begin to weigh on me more than I can say—I need air. I feel overwhelmed by boredom and grief."

Almond Blossom, 1890

Vincent moved north to Auvers, a small town near Paris, where he could stay under a doctor-friend's supervision. On the way there, he visited Theo. Theo's wife had just had a baby, whom they named Vincent. Brother Vincent showed up with this painting under his arm as a birthday gift. Theo's wife later recalled, "I had expected a sick man, but here was a sturdy, broad-shouldered man with a healthy color, a smile on his face, and a very resolute appearance."

This pietà creates a mystical mood.

The fleeting glory of the *Almond Blossom*

In his new surroundings, he continued painting, averaging a canvas a day, but was interrupted by spells that swung from boredom to madness. His letters to Theo were generally optimistic, but he worried that he'd soon succumb completely to insanity and never paint again.

▶ *Vincent's final landscapes are walls of bright, thick paint. Nature is charged from within with a swirling energy.*

Wheat Field with Crows, 1890

This new attack...came on me in the fields, on a windy day, when I was busy painting.

On July 27, 1890, Vincent left his room, walked out to a nearby field, and put a bullet through his chest.

This is one of the last paintings Vincent finished. We can try to search the wreckage of his life for the black box explaining what happened, but there's not much there. His life was sad and tragic, but the record he left is one not of sadness, but of beauty—intense beauty. The windblown wheat field is a nest of restless energy. Scenes like this must have overwhelmed Vincent with their incredible beauty—too much, too fast, with no release. The sky is stormy and dark blue, almost nighttime, barely lit by two suns boiling through the deep ocean of blue. The road starts nowhere, leads nowhere, disappearing into the burning wheat field. Above all of this swirling beauty fly the crows, the dark ghosts that had hovered over his life since the cemetery in Nuenen.

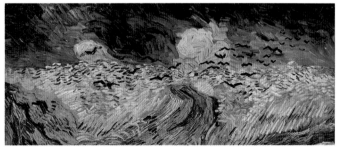

Vincent's last painting is of a field, like the one where he would end his short life.

Red Light District Walk

Amsterdam's oldest neighborhood has hosted the world's oldest profession since the Middle Ages. Today, prostitution and public marijuana use thrive here, creating a spectacle that's unique in all of Europe.

On our walk, we'll see history, sleaze, and cheese: prostitutes in windows, drunks in doorways, cruising packs of foreign twenty-somethings, and cannabis being enjoyed. The main event is sex: prostitutes in bras, thongs, and high heels, standing in window displays, offering their bodies—and it's all legal.

Not for Everyone: The Red Light District seems to have something to offend everyone. Whether it's in-your-face images of graphic sex, exploited immigrant women, whips and chains, passed-out drug addicts, the pungent smells of pot smoke and urine, or just the shameless commercialism of it all, it's not everyone's cup of tea. And, although I encourage people to expand their horizons, it's also perfectly OK to say, "No, thank you."

ORIENTATION

Length of This Walk: Allow two hours.

Photography: Don't take photos of women in windows—even with an inconspicuous phone camera—or a snarly bouncer may appear from out of nowhere to forcibly rip it from your hands. Photos of landmarks are OK, but remember that a camera or phone makes a prime target in this high-theft area.

When to Go: The best times to visit are afternoons and early evenings. Avoid late nights (after about 22:30), when the tourists disappear and the area gets creepy.

Safety: The neighborhood is slowly gentrifying, with trendy restaurants and boutiques, and there are plenty of police on horseback keeping things orderly. But there are also plenty of rowdy drunks, drug-pushing lowlifes, con artists, and pickpockets. Assume any fight or commotion is a ploy to distract innocent victims who are about to lose their wallets.

Old Church (Oude Kerk): Church—€12, Mon-Sat 10:00-18:00, Sun 13:00-17:30; tower climb—€9 with 30-minute tour in English, April-Oct departs on the half-hour Mon-Sat 12:00-18:00, none Sun or off-season.

Prostitution Information Center (PIC): Wed-Sat 12:00-17:00, closed Sun-Tue, +31 20 420 7328, www.pic-amsterdam.com.

Tours: While guided tours are not allowed in the Red Light District, the Prostitution Information Center gives educational **"Walk & Talk"** tours several times a week (€25, Wed-Sat at 17:00, +31 20 420 7328, for details and to sign up visit www.pic-amsterdam. com). The "tour" begins with a talk in their shop. Next, they give you a proposed self-guided walking route. Afterward, there's a follow-up meeting with a sex worker back in their office.

🎧 Download my free Red Light District **audio tour.**

Our Lord in the Attic Museum: €15.50, Mon-Fri 10:00-17:00, Sat until 18:00, Sun 13:00-18:00.

Erotic Museum: €7, daily 11:00-24:00.

Red Light Secrets Museum of Prostitution: €14.50; Sun-Thu 11:00-22:00, Fri-Sat until 23:00, www.redlightsecrets.com.

Cannabis College: Free, daily 11:00-18:00.

Hemp Gallery and Hash, Marijuana, and Hemp Museum: €10, includes audioguide, daily 10:00-22:00.

THE WALK BEGINS

▶ *Start on Dam Square. Face the big, fancy Grand Hotel Krasnapolsky. To the left of the hotel stretches the long street called...*

❶ Warmoesstraat

You're walking along one of the city's oldest streets. It's the traditional border of the Red Light District.

▶ *Our first stop is the small shop with the large, yellow triangle sign, about 100 yards down on the right at #141.*

❷ Condomerie

Located at the entrance to the Red Light District, this is the perfect place to get prepared. Besides selling an amazing variety of condoms, this shop has a knack for entertainment, working to make their front-window display appropriate to the season. Pop in and look around.

▶ *From here, pass the two little street barricades with cute red lights around them and enter the traffic-free world of...*

❸ De Wallen

Amsterdammers call this area De Wallen ("The Walls"), after the old retaining walls that once stood here. It's the oldest part of town, with the oldest church. It grew up between the harbor and Dam Square, where the city was born. Amsterdam was a port town, located where the river met the sea. The city traded in all kinds of goods, including things popular with sailors and businessmen away from home—like sex and drugs.

According to legend, Quentin Tarantino holed up at a hotel here

Condom shop—be prepared   Smartshops sell natural hallucinogens.

for three months in 1993 to write *Pulp Fiction*. The neighborhood attracts many out-of-towners, especially Brits. They catch cheap flights here for "stag" (bachelor) parties or just a wild weekend—and the Dutch accommodate them with Irish pubs and soccer matches on TVs in the bars.

► *Continue down Warmoesstraat a few more steps. At #97 is the...*

❹ Elements of Nature Smartshop

This "smartshop" is a clean, well-lit, fully professional retail outlet that sells powerful drugs, many of which are illegal in America. Products are clearly marked with prices, brief descriptions, ingredients, and effects. The knowledgeable salespeople can give you more information on their "100 percent natural products that play with the human senses."

Their "natural" drugs include harmless nutrition boosters (such as royal jelly), harmful but familiar tobacco, and herbal versions of popular dance-club drugs (such as herbal Ecstasy). Marijuana seeds are the big sellers.

► *Continue a bit farther down Warmoesstraat, to an area filled with...*

❺ Sex Shops

A few steps down Warmoesstraat, at #89, was **Mr. B's** Leather and Rubber Land, proudly flying an S&M flag. It's now Jamin, a candy store. Yes, things are changing—but **DD** (Dirty Dicks) across the street at #86 is still in business. Throughout the district, various sex-shop retail outlets deal in erotic paraphernalia (dildos, S&M starter kits, kinky magazines) and offer video booths with porn films. While Amsterdam is notorious for its Red Light District, even small Dutch towns often have a sex shop and a brothel to satisfy their citizens' needs.

► *Backtrack a few steps to the intersection and head down Wijde Kerksteeg to the...*

❻ Old Church (Oude Kerk)

As the name implies, this was the medieval city's original church. Returning from a long sea voyage, sailors of yore would spy the steeple of the Old Church on the horizon and know they were home. Having returned safely, they'd come here to give thanks to St. Nicholas—the patron saint of this church, of seafarers, of Christmas, and of the city of Amsterdam.

Church construction began in the early 1200s—starting with a humble wooden chapel that expanded into a stone structure by the time it was consecrated in 1306. It was added onto in fits and starts for the next 200 years—as is apparent in the building's many gangly parts. Then, in the 15th century, Amsterdam built the New Church (Nieuwe Kerk) on Dam Square. But the Old Church still had the tallest spire, the biggest organ, and the most side-altars, and remained the city's center of activity, bustling inside and out with merchants and street markets.

The **tower** is 290 feet high, with an octagonal steeple atop a bell tower (you can pay to climb to the top). This tower served as the model for many other Dutch steeples. The carillon has 47 bells, which can chime mechanically or be played by one of Amsterdam's three official carillonneurs.

Circle to the right to the church entrance. While the church is historic, the **interior** doesn't offer much to see other than hundreds of gravestones in the floor (the most famous is for Rembrandt's wife, Saskia).

In the 16th century, the church, permanently stripped of "pope-ish" decoration, was transformed from Catholic to Dutch Reformed, "St. Nicholas" was dropped from the name, and it became known by the nickname everyone called it anyway—the Old Church. Nowadays, the church is the holy needle around which the unholy Red Light District spins.

Back outside, explore around the right side of the church. You'll see a statue dedicated to the **Unknown Prostitute.** She's nicknamed

Old Church—historic charm amid the sleaze

Statue honoring the Unknown Prostitute

Red Light District Walk

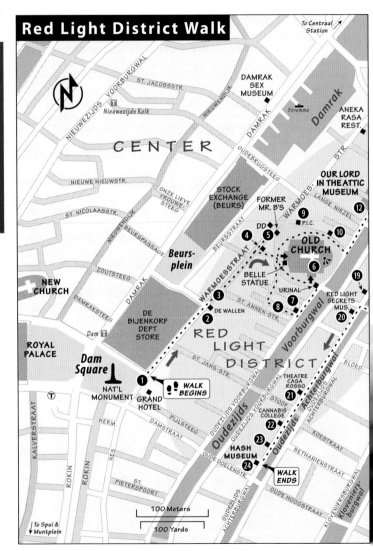

To Centraal Station

DAMRAK SEX MUSEUM

Stromma

ANEKA RASA REST.

ST. JACOBSSTR.

NIEUWEZIJDS VOORBURGWAL

NIEUWENDIJK

Nieuwezijds Kolk

DAMRAK

DAMRAK

CENTER

OUDEBRUGSTEEG

OUR LORD IN THE ATTIC MUSEUM

NIEUWE NIEUWSTR.

ONZE LIEVE VROUWE STEEG

ST. NICOLAASSTR.

NIEUWENDIJK

NIEUWE BEURSPASSAGE

STOCK EXCHANGE (BEURS)

FORMER MR. B'S

WARMOES STR.

LANGE NIEZEL

⑫

⑨ P.I.C.

DD ◆

Beurs-plein

ZOUTSTEEG

BEURSSTRAAT

④

⑤

OLD CHURCH

⑩

NEW CHURCH

DAMRAKSTEEG

WARMOESSTRAAT

BELLE STATUE

⑥

⑲

ROYAL PALACE

DE BIJENKORF DEPT STORE

Dam

③

DE WALLEN

②

ST. ANNEN-STR.

URINAL

⑧ ⑦

RED LIGHT SECRETS MUS.

⑳

Dam Square

RED LIGHT

Voorburgwal

KALVERSTRAAT

NAT'L MONUMENT

①

WALK BEGINS

ST. JANS-STR.

DISTRICT

Achterburgwal

BLOED...

GRAND HOTEL

OUDEZIJDS VOORBURGWAL

STOO...

THEATRE CASA ROSSO

⑳

⑳

Oudezijds

HERM.

DAMSTRAAT

OUDEZIJDS VOORBURGWAL

CANNABIS COLLEGE

⑳

Achterburgwal

KOESTRAAT

ROKIN

NES

PIJLSTEEG

⑳

HASH MUSEUM

⑳

Oudezijds

OUDEZIJDS ACHTERBURGWAL

BETHANIENSTRAAT

ROKIN

ST. PIETERSPOORT

WALK ENDS

OUDE DOELENSTR.

OUDE HOOGSTRAAT

Kloveniersburgwal

To Spui & Muntplein

100 Meters

100 Yards

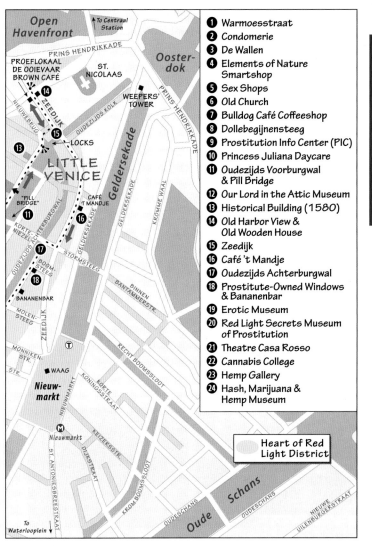

1 Warmoesstraat
2 Condomerie
3 De Wallen
4 Elements of Nature Smartshop
5 Sex Shops
6 Old Church
7 Bulldog Café Coffeeshop
8 Dollebegijnensteeg
9 Prostitution Info Center (PIC)
10 Princess Juliana Daycare
11 Oudezijds Voorburgwal & Pill Bridge
12 Our Lord in the Attic Museum
13 Historical Building (1580)
14 Old Harbor View & Old Wooden House
15 Zeedijk
16 Café 't Mandje
17 Oudezijds Achterburgwal
18 Prostitute-Owned Windows & Bananenbar
19 Erotic Museum
20 Red Light Secrets Museum of Prostitution
21 Theatre Casa Rosso
22 Cannabis College
23 Hemp Gallery
24 Hash, Marijuana & Hemp Museum

Heart of Red Light District

Belle, and the statue honors "sex workers around the world." Attached to the church like barnacles are **small buildings.** These were originally used as homes for priests, church offices, or rental units. The house to the right of the entrance is now a delightful café (de Koffie Schenkerij).

The green metal structure over by the canal is a public **urinal.** It offers just enough privacy.

▶ *From the urinal, go a half-block south along the canal toward the...*

➐ Bulldog Café Coffeeshop

The Bulldog claims to be Amsterdam's very first marijuana coffeeshop, established here in 1975. Now there's a chain of Bulldogs around the city.

As coffeeshops go, the Bulldog is considered pretty touristy, catering to a young crowd. (Older connoisseurs often seek out smaller places with better-quality pot.) The staff is unintimidating, though, and timid first-timers are guided through the process. Step in and snoop around. As long as you don't take photos, you're welcome.

The political winds regarding cannabis are always shifting. Some Dutch leaders propose forbidding sales to nonresidents, hoping to discourage European drug dealers from buying pot to sell illegally in their home countries. However, such a law would be devastating for businesses that depend on out-of-towners, so many Amsterdam politicians favor keeping pot legal.

▶ *Time to dive into the heart of the Red Light District. On either side of the Bulldog are long, skinny lanes with big windows. Walk down the one to the left called...*

Marijuana coffeeshop—no big deal here

Busy Red Light District alley

❽ Dollebegijnensteeg

This was once the thick of Amsterdam's high-density prostitution scene. What was until recently a can-can of sex workers flirting in their windows is now pretty empty as the city works to strategically contain and limit the sex trade. Imagine how it appeared until a couple years ago: Window after window of women in panties and bras would wink at prospective customers, rap on the window to attract attention, text their friends, or look disdainfully at sightseers.

▸ *At the cross street, turn right to return to the Old Church. Circle the church clockwise. Around the side, at Enge Kerksteeg 3, is the...*

❾ Prostitution Information Center (PIC)

This center (a nonprofit run by donations) exists to demystify prostitution, giving visitors matter-of-fact information on how the trade works and what it's like to be a sex worker. It doles out pamphlets, books, condoms, T-shirts, and other offbeat souvenirs, and offers self-guided "Walk & Talk" tours (see "Orientation," earlier, for details). They have a map showing exactly where prostitution is legal, and sell a small, frank booklet answering the most common questions tourists have about Amsterdam's Red Light District

Next door is a room-rental office (#3, *Kamerverhuurbedrijf*). Prostitutes come here to rent window space and bedrooms to use for their work. The office also sells work supplies—condoms by the case, toilet tissue, and lubricants. This office does not arrange sex. The women who rent space from this business are self-employed and negotiate directly with their customers.

In return for their rental fees, prostitutes get security. The rental office provides constant video surveillance. (You may see small

Red Light areas have strict security video.

The "PIC" has info about the sex trade.

cameras and orange alarm lights above many windows.) If prostitutes encounter trouble, they press a buzzer that swiftly calls a burly bouncer or the police. While the area may look rough, aside from tricky pickpockets these streets are actually pretty safe.

▶ *Continue circling clockwise around the church and find the brick building on the left at Oudekerksplein 8. This is the...*

⑩ Princess Juliana Daycare

De Wallen is also a residential neighborhood, where ordinary citizens go about their daily lives. Of course, locals need someplace to send their kids. The Princess Juliana Daycare is for newborns to four-year-olds. It was built in the 1970s, when the idea was to mix all dimensions of society together, absorbing the seedy into the decent. I don't know about you, but this location would be a tough sell where I come from.

▶ *Turn left at the canal and continue north along...*

⑪ Oudezijds Voorburgwal and Pill Bridge

Pause at "Pill Bridge" and enjoy the canal and all the old buildings with their charming gables. Back in the 1970s, this bridge was nicknamed for the retail items sold by the seedy guys who used to hang out here. Thanks to smart and pragmatic public policy, the Dutch have made great gains in fighting hard-drug addiction. And now this neighborhood is a pleasant place for a photo op.

▶ *Just past the bridge, at Oudezijds Voorburgwal 38, is one of the city's most worthwhile museums.*

⑫ Our Lord in the Attic Museum

With its triangular gable, this building looks like just another townhouse. But inside, it holds a secret—a small, lavishly decorated place of worship hidden in the attic. Although Amsterdam has long been known for its tolerance, back in the 16th and 17th centuries there was one group they kept in the closet—Catholics. (For more information, see page 133.)

▶ *Beyond the next bridge, on your left at #14, is an old brick building with red shutters.*

⑬ Historical Building

As we stroll up the canal, remember that this neighborhood is

Prostitution 101

The prostitutes here are self-employed—renting space and running their own business. They usually work a four- to eight-hour shift. A good spot costs about €100 for a day shift and €180 for an evening. Prostitutes are required to keep their premises hygienic, make sure their clients use condoms, and avoid minors. Rooms look tiny from the street, but these are just display windows. There's a bigger room behind or upstairs that comes with a bed, a sink, and not much else (or so I've heard). The average time for a visit: about 10 minutes.

While the hope here is that sex workers are smartly regulated small-businesspeople, in reality the line between victim and entrepreneur is not always clear. Although some women choose sex work as a lucrative career, others (some say most) are forced into it by circumstance—poverty, drug addiction, abusive men, and immigration scams. Though there are male prostitutes, they solicit work mostly online and in clubs.

Popular sex workers can make about €1,000 a day. The law, not pimps, protects them, and they fill out tax returns. As shocking as legalized prostitution may seem to some, it's a good example of a pragmatic Dutch solution to an age-old dilemma.

With a vision of "gentrification by design," Amsterdam's city government is splicing in other "legitimate" businesses into a district that for centuries has relied on only one product. A major Red Light District landlord was essentially given the option either to lease many of his booths to the city or be zoned out of business. The city picked up the leases, and windows that once showcased "girls for rent" now showcase mannequins wearing the latest fashions—lit by lights that aren't red.

Amsterdam's oldest. It sits on formerly marshy land that was reclaimed by diking off the sea's tidal surge. That location gave Amsterdam's merchants easy access to both river trade and the North Sea. This building dates from that era—around 1580.

The part of the canal we're walking along now is known as **"Little Venice"** (a term used Europe-wide for any charming neighborhood with canalside houses). Houses rise directly from the water here, with no quays or streets.

▶ *Continue straight up a small, inclined lane called Sint Olofssteeg. At the top, turn left and walk along the street called Zeedijk. Go about 100 yards to the end of the block, where it opens up to an...*

⑭ Old Harbor View and Old Wooden House

As you survey the urban scene of today's Damrak and Centraal station, imagine the scene as it looked in the 1600s. What today is mostly concrete was once the city's harbor. Ocean-going ships sailed in and out of the harbor through an opening located where the train station sits now (on reclaimed land).

The **old wooden house** near here (at Zeedijk 1, now a café) was once a tavern, sitting right at what was then the water's edge.

Picture a ship tying up in the harbor. The crew has just returned home from a two-year voyage to Bali. They're bringing home fabulous riches—crates and crates of spices, coffee, and silk. Sailors are celebrating their homecoming, spilling onto Zeedijk. Here they'll be greeted by swinging ladies swinging red lanterns. Their first stop might be nearby St. Olaf's chapel to say a prayer of thanks—or perhaps they'll head straight to this tavern at Zeedijk 1 and drop anchor for a good Dutch beer. *Ahh-hh!*

Pill Bridge, near quaint Little Venice

Pioneering gay bar along Zeedijk street

▸ *But our journey continues. Backtrack along the same street, to the crest of a bridge, on...*

ⓑ Zeedijk

The waterway below you is part of the city's system of **locks:** Once upon a time, each day a worker would open up the locks and the tide would flush out the city's canals.

In the early 1600s, this neighborhood was thriving with overseas trade. But Amsterdam would soon lose its maritime supremacy to England and France, and De Wallen never really recovered. By the 1970s, Zeedijk had become unbelievably sleazy. The area was a no-man's-land of junkies fighting among themselves, and the police just kept their distance.

But locals longed to take back this historic corner of their city and got to work. First, they legalized marijuana and then they cracked down on hard drugs—heroin, cocaine, and pills. Almost overnight, the illicit-drug trade dropped dramatically. Dealers got stiff sentences. Addicts got treatment. Decades later, the policy seemed to have worked. Zeedijk belonged to the people of Amsterdam once again—only later to be taken over by tourists. Today there's a push to remind visitors that, yes, real people live here.

▸ *Continue down Zeedijk and around the bend. Pause at #63, on the left.*

⓰ Café 't Mandje

This is one of Europe's first gay bars. It opened in 1927, closed in 1985, and is now a working bar once again. It stands as a memorial to the woman who ran it during its heyday in the 1950s and '60s: Bet van Beeren. Bet was a lesbian, and her bar became a hangout for gay people. Neckties hang from the ceiling, a reminder of Bet's tradition of scissoring off customers' ties.

▸ *Continuing down Zeedijk street, make the next right and head a few steps down narrow Korte Stormsteeg street, back to the canalside red lights. Go left, walking along the left side of the canal.*

⓱ Oudezijds Achterburgwal

We're back in the quirky glow of the Red Light District. This beautiful, tree-lined canal is the heart of this neighborhood's nightlife, playing host to most of the main nightclubs.

Social Control

De Wallen has pioneered the Dutch concept of "social control." In Holland, neighborhood security doesn't come from just the police, but from neighbors looking out for each another. If Geert doesn't buy bread for two days, the baker asks around if anyone's seen him. An elderly man feels safe in his home, knowing he's being watched over by the prostitutes next door. Unlike many big cities, there's no chance that anyone here could die or be in trouble and go unnoticed. Video-surveillance cameras keep an eye on the streets. So do prostitutes, who buzz for help if they spot trouble. As you stroll, watch the men who watch the women who watch out for their neighbors—"social control."

▶ *Start making your way down the street's left-hand side. After about 30 yards, pause at the small alleyway called Boomsteeg.*

⓲ Prostitute-Owned Windows and Bananenbar

Many of the prostitution windows near here (Oudezijds #17, #19, and #27) are run by a cooperative of entrepreneurial prostitutes to create nice rooms for their clients and good working conditions for themselves—such as a lounge for sex workers between shifts.

Continue a few yards ahead, to #37. This popular nightclub ("Banana Bar") is a strip club with a-peel: For €60 you get admission for an hour, drinks included. Undressed ladies perch on the bar and serve the drinks. Touching is not allowed, but you can order a banana and the lady will serve it to you, any way you like.

▶ *At Molensteeg, cross the bridge and look to the right.*

⓳ Erotic Museum

If it's graphic sex you seek, this is not the place. To put it bluntly, this museum is not very good (the Damrak Sex Museum described on page 132 is better). However, it does offer a peek at some of the sex services found in the Red Light District. Displays include reconstructions of a prostitute's chambers, sex-shop windows, and videos of nightclub sex shows (on the third floor).

▶ *From the bridge, turn left and walk south along Oudezijds Achterburg-wal. At #60H is the...*

⓴ Red Light Secrets Museum of Prostitution

Though overpriced, this museum is an earnest and mildly educational behind-the-scenes look at prostitution. You'll walk through a typical (tiny) room where prostitutes stand at the window, and a typical (tiny) back room with a bed and sink. Perhaps most thought provoking: a video giving you the point of view of a sex worker as browsers check you out.

▶ *Continuing south, you'll pass two Casa Rosso franchises a block apart. The larger, lined by pink elephants, is...*

㉑ Theatre Casa Rosso

This is the Red Light District's best-known nightclub for live sex shows. Audience members pay a single price that includes drinks and a show (€50). On stage are naked people engaging in sex acts—some simulated, some completely real.

As you continue south along the canal, you gotta wonder, "Why does Amsterdam embrace prostitution and drugs?" It's not that the Dutch are more liberal in their attitudes. They're simply more prag-matic. They've found that when the sex trade goes underground, you

Scenic canals and sex shows

get pimps, mobsters, and the spread of STDs. When marijuana is illegal, you get drug dealers, gangs, and violent turf wars. Their solution is to minimize problems through strict regulation.

▶ *But enough about sex. Let's talk about drugs. Along the right side of the next block, you'll find several cannabis-related establishments.*

㉒ Cannabis College

This free, nonprofit public study center aims to explain the pros and cons (but mostly pros) of the industrial, medicinal, and recreational uses of the green stuff. You can read about practical hemp products, the medical uses of marijuana, and police prosecution/persecution of cannabis users. For a €3 donation, you can visit the organic flowering cannabis garden.

▶ *Continue up the street to #130, the...*

㉓ Hemp Gallery

One ticket admits you to both the Hemp Gallery and the Hash, Marijuana, and Hemp Museum (described next). If you have the patience to read its thorough displays, you'll learn plenty about how

In the evening, the area is safe and festive.

Several sights teach about marijuana...   ...and its notorious history.

valuable cannabis was to Holland during its golden age. The leafy green plant was grown on large plantations. The fibrous stalks (hemp) were made into rope and canvas for ships, and even used to make clothing and lace. Without hemp, Henry Hudson would never have made it out of the harbor.

▶ *Next is our last stop at #148, the...*

㉔ Hash, Marijuana, and Hemp Museum

This museum treats marijuana like it deserves scholarly study. The exhibits are quite extensive and interesting. The highlight is the flowering room, where you look through windows at live cannabis plants in bloom. At a certain stage they're "sexed" to weed out the boring males and "selected" to produce the most powerful strains. At the museum's exit you'll pass through the **Sensi Seed Bank Store,** which sells weed seeds, how-to books, and knickknacks geared to growers.

Congratulations

We've seen a lot—from sex workers to drug pushers to the ghosts of pioneer lesbians to politically active heads with green thumbs. We've talked a bit of history, a little politics, and a lot of sleaze. Congratulations. You've survived. Now, go back to your hotel and take a shower.

Jordaan Walk

This walk takes you from Dam Square—the bustling center of Amsterdam—to the Anne Frank House, and then deep into the characteristic Jordaan (yor-DAHN) neighborhood. Cafés, boutiques, bookstores, and art galleries have gentrified the area. On this cultural scavenger hunt, you'll experience the laid-back Dutch lifestyle and catch a few intimate details that most busy tourists never appreciate. You'll see things in the Jordaan that are commonplace in no other city in the world.

Allow about 1.5 hours for this short and easygoing walk—nice in the sleepy morning or en route to a Jordaan dinner in the evening. (But Sundays aren't ideal, as many shops and St. Andrew's Courtyard are closed.) Be prepared to enjoy some of Amsterdam's most charming canal scenes.

🎧 Download my free Jordaan Walk audio tour.

THE WALK BEGINS

❶ Dam Square

Start in Dam Square, where the city was born (for more on this square, see page 22). The original residents settled east of here, in the De Wallen neighborhood (now the Red Light District). But as Amsterdam grew—from a river-trading village to a worldwide seagoing empire—the population needed new places to live. Citizens started reclaiming land to the west of Dam Square and built a "new church" (Nieuwe Kerk) to serve these new neighborhoods. Over time they needed still more land and continued to push westward. Canal by canal, they created waterways lined with merchants' townhouses.

By the 1600s—Amsterdam's golden age—residents had moved even farther west, building an even newer church called the Westerkerk (Western Church). The residential neighborhood around it is what we'll explore on this walk—the Jordaan.

▶ *Facing the Royal Palace, slip (to the right) between the palace and New Church. Check out the red-and-white brick building—the* **Magna Plaza mall.** *When it was built in 1899, it was Amsterdam's main post*

Start on Dam Square, face west, and walk.

office and was constructed atop a foundation of thousands of pilings. Facing Magna Plaza, head right, walking 50 yards down the busy street to the corner of a tiny street called…

❷ Molsteeg

Scan the higgledy-piggledy facades along the busy street. Are you drunk, high…or just in Amsterdam, where the houses were built on mud? Check out the nice line of gables in this row of houses.

Before moving on, notice the T-shirt gallery on the corner. Decades ago, I bought a Mark Raven T-shirt from a street vendor. Now this Amsterdam original has his own upscale shop, selling T-shirts and paintings featuring spindly lined, semi-abstract cityscapes.

▶ *Now head left down tiny Molsteeg street—but don't walk on the reddish pavement in the middle; that's for bikes. From here this tour's essentially a straight shot west, although the street changes names along the way.*

A few steps along, on the left, find house #5: It's from 1644. Just one window wide, it's typical of the city's narrow old merchants' houses, with a shop on the ground floor, living space in the middle, and storage in the attic. Look up to see the hooks above warehouse doors. Houses like this lean out toward the street on purpose, so you can hoist cargo (or a sofa) without banging it against the house.

At the intersection with Spuistraat, you'll likely see rows of **bicycles** parked along the street. Amsterdam's 850,000 residents own nearly that many bikes. Many people own two—a long-distance racing bike and an in-city bike, often deliberately kept in poor maintenance so it's less enticing to bike thieves. Locals are diligent about locking their bikes twice: They lock the spokes with the first lock and then chain the bike to something immovable, such as a city hitching rack.

Amsterdam is a great bike town—and indeed, bikes outnumber cars. The efficient Dutch appreciate a self-propelled machine that travels five times faster than a person on foot, while creating zero pollution, noise, parking problems, or high fuel costs. On a *fiets* (bike), a speedy local can traverse the historic center in about 10 minutes. Biking seems to keep the populace fit and good-looking—people here say that Amsterdam's health clubs are more for networking than for working out.

▶ *Cross what was another canal. After one more block, the street opens*

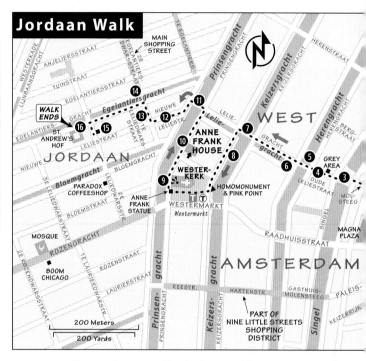

Jordaan Walk

onto a small space that's actually a bridge, straddling the Singel canal. It's called…

❸ Torensluis Bridge

We haven't quite reached the Jordaan yet, but the atmosphere already seems miles away from busy Dam Square. With cafés, art galleries, and fine benches for picnics, this is a great place to relax and take in a golden age atmosphere.

Singel Canal: This canal was the original moat running around the old walled city. This bridge is so wide because it was the road that led to one of the original city gates.

Houses: The area still looks much as it might have during the Dutch golden age of the 1600s, when Amsterdam's seagoing merchants

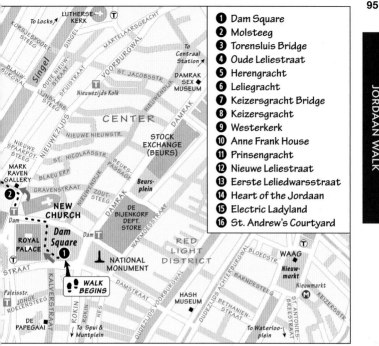

1. Dam Square
2. Molsteeg
3. Torensluis Bridge
4. Oude Leliestraat
5. Herengracht
6. Leliegracht
7. Keizersgracht Bridge
8. Keizersgracht
9. Westerkerk
10. Anne Frank House
11. Prinsengracht
12. Nieuwe Leliestraat
13. Eerste Leliedwarsstraat
14. Heart of the Jordaan
15. Electric Ladyland
16. St. Andrew's Courtyard

ruled the waves. Fueled with wealth, the city quickly became a major urban center, filled with impressive homes.

The houses crowd together, shoulder-to-shoulder. They're built on top of thousands of logs hammered vertically into the marshy soil to provide a foundation. Over the years, they've shifted with the tides, leaving some leaning this way and that. Notice that some of the brick houses have iron rods strapped onto the sides. These act like braces, binding the bricks to an inner skeleton of wood. Almost all Amsterdam houses have big, tall windows to let in as much light as possible.

Although some houses look quite narrow, most of them extend far back. The rear of the building—called the *achterhuis*—is often much more spacious than you might expect, judging from a skinny facade.

Multatuli: The "big head" statue honors a writer known by his

Playful Jordaan residents   Torensluis Bridge—cafés and views

pen name, Multatuli. Born in Amsterdam in 1820, Multatuli (a.k.a. Eduard Douwes Dekker) did what many young Dutchmen did back then: He sought his fortune in the East Indies, then a colony of the Netherlands. He witnessed firsthand the hard life of Javanese natives slaving away on Dutch-owned plantations. His semi-autobiographical novel, *Max Havelaar* (1860), follows a progressive civil servant fighting to reform colonial abuses. He was the first author to criticize Dutch colonial practices.

Locks: In the distance, way down at the north end of the Singel, beyond the dome, you can glimpse one of the canal's locks. Those white-flagpole thingies, sprouting at 45-degree angles, are part of the apparatus that opens and shuts the gates. While the canals originated as a way to drain diked-off marshland, they eventually became part of the city's sewer system. They were flushed daily: Just open the locks and let the North Sea tides come in and out.

The Dutch are credited with inventing locks in the 1300s. (Let's not ask the Chinese.) Besides controlling water flow in the city, they allow ships to pass from higher to lower water levels, and vice versa. It's because of locks that you can ship something by boat from here inland. From this very spot, you could hop a boat and go upriver, connect to the Rhine, and eventually—over the continental divide in Germany—connect to the Danube and then sail to Romania and the Black Sea.

▶ *Continue west on...*

❹ Oude Leliestraat

"Old Lily Street" is the well-worn path for tourists going to the Anne

Gables

Along the rooftops, Amsterdam's famous gables are false fronts to enhance roofs that are, generally, sharply pitched. Gables come in all shapes and sizes. They could be ornamented with animal and human heads, garlands, urns, scrolls, and curlicues. Despite their infinite variety, most belong to a few distinct types. See how many of these you can spot.

A simple "point" gable just follows the triangular shape of a normal pitched roof. A "bell" gable is shaped like...well, guess. "Step" gables are triangular in shape and lined with steps. The one with a rectangular protrusion at the peak is called a "spout" gable. "Neck" gables rise up vertically from a pair of sloping "shoulders." "Cornice" gables make pointed roofs look classically horizontal. (There's probably even a "clark" gable, but frankly, I don't give a damn.)

Point

Bell

Step

Spout

Neck

Cornice

Frank House and is therefore lined with shops catering not to locals but to tourists. And one of those shops sells marijuana.

The **Grey Area** is a thriving coffeeshop; like Holland's other "coffeeshops," it sells pot. The green-and-white decal in the window identifies it as #092 in the city's licensing program. While smoking marijuana is essentially legal here, the café's name refers to the murky back side of the marijuana business—how coffeeshops get their supply from wholesalers. That's the "gray area" that Dutch laws have yet to sort out.

This esteemed coffeeshop, which works with the best boutique growers in Holland, regularly wins big at Amsterdam's annual Cannabis Cup Awards—a "high" honor, to be sure.

▶ *The next canal is…*

❺ Herengracht

Amsterdam added this canal during its golden age boom in the 1600s. It's named for the *heren,* the wealthy city merchants who lined it with their mansions. Even today, Herengracht runs through a high-rent district. (Zoning here forbids houseboats.)

Check out the house that's kitty-corner across the bridge, at Herengracht 150. It has features you'll find on many old Amsterdam buildings. On the roof, rods support the false-front gable. From this side view, you can see that, though a townhouse might have a narrow entrance, it can stretch far back from the street.

▶ *Continue west, walking along…*

❻ Leliegracht

This is one of the city's prettiest small canals (at least when its

Leliegracht canal is short and sweet.

Herengracht—a canal of gabled townhouses

embankments aren't being rebuilt), lined with trees and lanterns, and crossed by a series of arched bridges. There are some 400 such bridges in Amsterdam. It's a pleasant street of eccentric boutiques, trendy furniture shops, and bookstores. Notice that some buildings have staircases leading down below the street level to residences. Looking up, you'll see the characteristic beams jutting out from the top with a cargo-hoisting hook on the end. The view from a bay window here must be exceptional.

▶ *Continue on to the next canal, and pause on the* ❼ *Keizersgracht Bridge. Take in another fine row of gables and the colorfully crowned tower of the Westerkerk—where we're headed. After the bridge, we'll take a detour off our westward route and veer left along...*

❽ Keizersgracht

Walk south about 100 yards along the canal.

Homomonument: You'll reach a set of steps leading down to the water, where a triangular pink stone juts into the canal. This is part of the so-called Homomonument—a memorial to homosexuals who lost their lives in World War II, and a commemoration of all those persecuted for their sexuality. The pink triangle is just one corner of a larger triangle that forms the Homomonument. (The pink-triangle design reclaims the symbol that the Nazis used to mark homosexuals.) You may see flowers or cards left here by friends and loved ones.

Westermarkt Square: Walk through the square called Westermarkt, between the church and busy Raadhuisstraat. You'll pass several very Dutch kiosks. The first, called Pink Point, gives out information on gay and lesbian Amsterdam, especially nightlife. The next sells french fries; when it's closed, the shutters feature funny paintings putting *friets* into great masterpieces of Western art.

▶ *Keep walking toward the entrance to...*

❾ Westerkerk (Western Church)

Near the western end of the church, look for a cute little statue. It's of Anne Frank, who holed up with her family in a house just down the block from here.

Now, look up at the towering spire of the impressive Westerkerk. The crown shape was a gift of the Habsburg emperor, Maximilian I. In thanks for a big loan, the city got permission to use the Habsburg royal

A memorial to AIDS victims
The crown of the Westerkerk

symbol. The tower also displays the symbol of Amsterdam, with its three Xs. The Westerkerk was built in 1631, as the city was expanding out from Dam Square. Rembrandt's buried inside...but no one knows where. You can pop into the church for free (generally open Mon-Sat 11:00-15:00, closed Sun; tower—closed for renovation, see page 129).

The church tower has a carillon that chimes every 15 minutes. At other times, it plays full songs. Invented by Dutch bellmakers in the 1400s, a carillon is a set of bells of different sizes and pitches. There's a live musician inside the tower who plays a keyboard to make the music. Mozart, Vivaldi, and Bach—all of whom lived during the heyday of the carillon—wrote music that sounds great on this unique instrument. During World War II, the Westerkerk's carillon played every day. This hopeful sound reminded Anne Frank that there was, indeed, an outside world.

▶ *Continue around the church and walk north along the Prinsengracht canal to #263. This doorway was the original entrance to the...*

❿ Anne Frank House

This was where the Frank family hid from the Nazis for 25 months. With actual artifacts, the museum gives the cold, mind-boggling statistics of fascism the all-important intimacy of a young girl who lived through it and died from it. Even unemotional types find themselves caught up in Anne's story. 📖 See the Anne Frank House Tour chapter.

▶ *At the next bridge, turn left. Stop at its high point, mid-canal, for a view of...*

⓫ Prinsengracht

The "Princes' Canal" runs through what's considered one of the most livable areas in town. It's lined with houseboats, some of the city's estimated 2,500. These small vessels were once cargo ships—but by the 1930s, they had become obsolete. They found a new use as houseboats lining the canals of Amsterdam, where dry land is so limited and pricey.

Today, former cargo holds are fashioned into elegant, cozy living rooms. The once-powerful engines have generally been removed to make more room for living space. Moorage spots are prized and grandfathered in, making some of the junky old boats worth more than you'd think. Houseboaters can plug hoses and cables into outlets along the canals to get water, sewer, and electricity.

▸ *The recommended **Café 't Smalle** is a block to the right. Once you cross Prinsengracht, you enter what's officially considered the Jordaan neighborhood. Facing west (toward Café de Prins), cross the bridge and veer left down...*

A statue to Anne Frank remembers those who hid from the Nazis in the back of a nearby house.

⑫ Nieuwe Leliestraat

Welcome to the quiet Jordaan. Built in the 1600s as a working-class housing area, it's now home to artists and yuppies. The name Jordaan probably was not derived from the French *jardin*—but given the neighborhood's garden-like ambience, it seems like it should have been.

Train your ultra-sharp "traveler's eyes" on all the tiny details of Amsterdam life. Notice how the pragmatic Dutch deal with junk mail. On the doors, stickers next to mail slots say *Nee* or *Ja* (no or yes), telling the postal worker if they'll accept or refuse junk mail. (A practical recent law made *Nee* the default, and residents now must request junk mail to get it...that's so Dutch.) Residents are allowed a "front-yard garden" as long as it's no more than one sidewalk tile wide. A speed bump in the road keeps things peaceful. The red metal bollards known as *Amsterdammertjes* ("little Amsterdammers") have been bashing balls since the 1970s, when they were put in to stop people from parking on the sidewalks. Though many apartments have windows right on the street, the neighbors don't stare and the residents don't care.

▶ *At the first intersection, turn right onto...*

⑬ Eerste Leliedwarsstraat

Pause and linger awhile on this tiny lane. Imagine the frustrations of home ownership here. If your house is considered "historic," you need special permission and lots of money to renovate.

On this street, you can see three different examples of renovation. At house #9, it was done cheap and dirty: A historic (but run-down) home was simply torn down and replaced with an inexpensive, functional building with modern heating and plumbing. At #5, there's no renovation at all. The owners were too poor (stuck with rent-control

Some residents live on houseboats.

Study the houses on Eerste Leliedwarsstraat.

tenants), and they missed the window of time when a cheap rebuild was allowed. At #2A (across the street), the owners obviously had the cash to do a first-class sprucing up—it looks historic but is fully modern inside. (In this case, it's the work of Yvonne, who loves plants and lives upstairs while making and selling her art on the ground-floor level.) Even newly renovated homes like this must preserve their funky leaning angles and original wooden beams. They're certainly nice to look at, but absolutely maddening for owners who don't have a lot of money to meet city standards.

▶ *Just ahead, walk out to the middle of the bridge over the next canal (Egelantiersgracht). This is what I think of as the...*

⓮ Heart of the Jordaan

For me, this bridge and its surroundings capture the essence of the Jordaan. Take it all in: the bookstores, art galleries, working artists' studios, and small cafés full of rickety tables. The quiet canal is lined with trees and old, narrow buildings with gables—classic Amsterdam.

Looking south toward the Westerkerk, you'll see a completely different view of the church than most tourists get. Framed by narrow streets, crossed with streetlamp wires, and looming over shoppers on bicycles—to me, this is the church in its best light.

Turning around and looking north, you'll see the street called Tweede Egelantiersdwarsstraat—the laid-back Jordaan neighborhood's main shopping-and-people street. If you venture down there, you'll find boutiques, galleries, antique stores, hair salons, and an enticing array of restaurants. You'll notice there are no chain stores. So, the neighborhood just stays cute...it fits that great Dutch word for cozy, *gezellig.*

See no reefer, hear no reefer at Grey Area.

Jordaan's greatest sight: everyday life

▶ *Now head west along the canal (Egelantiersgracht) to the next bridge, where you'll turn left onto Tweede Leliedwarsstraat, and walk a few steps to #5.*

⑮ Electric Ladyland

This small shop, with a flowery window display, calls itself "The First Museum of Fluorescent Art." Its funky facade hides an illuminated wonderland within, with a tiny exhibit of black-light art. It's the creation of Nick Padalino—one cool cat who really found his niche in life. He enjoys personally demonstrating the fluorescence found in unexpected places—everything from minerals to stamps to candy to the tattoo on his arm. Wow (€5; required 45-minute guided tours run Thu-Sat at 14:00, 15:00, 16:00, and 17:00; closed Sun-Wed; by appointment only via www.electricladyland.appointy.com).

After this tour, you might be interested in this little side trip: About 100 yards farther down the street and across the canal is the **Paradox Coffeeshop.** It's the perfect coffeeshop for the nervous American who wants a friendly, mellow place to go local—see page 152.

Nick welcomes you to his blacklight museum.

▶ *To reach our last stop, backtrack 20 paces from Electric Ladyland to the canal and turn left, then walk 20 yards to Egelantiersgracht #107, the entrance to...*

⑯ St. Andrew's Courtyard (Sint-Andrieshof)

The black door is marked *Sint-Andrieshof 107 t/m 145.* The doorway looks private, but it's the public entrance to a set of residences. It's generally open during daytime hours, except on Sundays. Enter quietly; you may have to push hard on the door. Go inside and continue through a blue-tile-lined passageway into a tiny garden courtyard (*hof*) surrounded by a dozen or so homes. This is one of the city's scores of similar *hofjes*—subsidized residences built around a courtyard and funded by churches, charities, and the city for low-income widows and pensioners. This one, from 1613, is one of the oldest in Amsterdam.

▶ *And this is where our walk ends—in a tranquil world that seems right out of a painting by Vermeer. You're just blocks from the bustle of Amsterdam, but it feels like another world. You're immersed in the Jordaan, where everything's in its place, where people—like Yvonne and Nick—find their place in life, and where life seems very good.*

Anne Frank House Tour

On May 10, 1940, Germany's Luftwaffe began bombing Schiphol Airport, preparing to invade the Netherlands. The Dutch army fought back, and the Nazis responded by leveling Rotterdam. Within a week, the Netherlands surrendered, Queen Wilhelmina fled to Britain, and Nazi soldiers goose-stepped past the Westerkerk and into Dam Square, where they draped huge swastikas on the Royal Palace. A five-year occupation began.

    The Anne Frank House immerses you, in a very immediate way, in the struggles and pains of the war years. Walk through rooms where, for two years, eight Amsterdam Jews hid from Nazi persecution. Though they were eventually discovered and all but one died in concentration camps, their story has an uplifting twist—the diary of Anne Frank, an affirmation of the human spirit that cannot be crushed.

ORIENTATION

Cost: €16, must book timed-entry ticket online in advance, includes excellent audioguide; €23 with 30-minute introduction in English.

Hours: Daily 9:00-22:00. Open every day except Yom Kippur.

Information: +31 20 556 7105, www.annefrank.org.

Advance Reservations Required: The Anne Frank House is both very popular and very small—and tickets sell out quickly. Tickets are only sold online. There are no tickets sold at the museum.

Plan to buy tickets nearly two months before your trip. Tickets are released online every Tuesday for visits the following six weeks. You'll choose between a standalone museum visit or a visit with a 30-minute introduction in English (the intro program tickets are easier to get).

If you have a **Museumkaart sightseeing pass,** entry is covered, but you must reserve an entry time online for €1. You can make this reservation even if you haven't purchased the pass yet—just be sure to buy the pass at another sight before your Anne Frank House visit.

Scam Alert: Don't buy tickets from scalpers. Tickets are only available at www.annefrank.org. Beware of third-party companies offering "Anne Frank House tours"—these do not include access to the house.

Getting There: It's at Prinsengracht 267. The museum entrance is around the corner, in the modern building at Westermarkt 20. Take tram #13 or #17 to the Westermarkt stop, about a block south of the museum's entrance.

What to Expect: You'll snake your way through the museum and point your audioguide at an activation point in each room. The house has many steep, narrow stairways that can be difficult for mobility-impaired visitors or young kids.

Length of This Tour: Allow one hour.

Baggage Check: Cloakroom for coats and small bags. No large bags are allowed.

Eating: The $$ museum café serves simple fare and has good views.

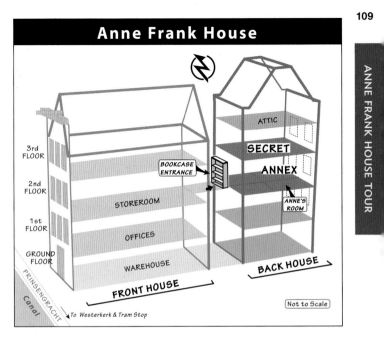

Anne Frank House

3rd FLOOR
2nd FLOOR
1st FLOOR
GROUND FLOOR

ATTIC
SECRET ANNEX
ANNE'S ROOM
BOOKCASE ENTRANCE
STOREROOM
OFFICES
WAREHOUSE

FRONT HOUSE
BACK HOUSE

PRINSENGRACHT Canal
To Westerkerk & Tram Stop

Not to Scale

THE TOUR BEGINS

We'll walk through the rooms where Anne Frank, her parents Otto and Edith, her sister Margot, and four other Jews hid for 25 months. The front half of the building, facing the canal, remained the offices and warehouses of an operating business. The back half, where the Franks and others lived, was the Secret Annex, its entrance concealed by a swinging bookcase.

▸ *After scanning your ticket, enter the ground-floor exhibit. Start with the important five-minute video (or 30-minute introduction). Then continue through a few more ground-floor rooms before going upstairs to the offices of the Franks' business.*

Otto Frank—Anne's father

Miep and Jan Gies helped the Franks hide.

First Floor Offices

From these rooms, Otto Frank ran a successful business called Opekta, selling spices and pectin for making jelly. When the Nazis gained power in Germany in 1933, Otto moved his family from Frankfurt to tolerant Amsterdam, hoping for a better life.

As the Nazis swarmed over the Netherlands, they were at first lenient toward, even friendly with, the vanquished Dutch. But soon they began imposing restrictions that affected one in ten Amsterdammers—that is, Jews. Jewish people were banned from movie theaters and trams, and even forbidden to ride bikes.

In February 1941, the Nazis started rounding up Amsterdam's Jews, shipping them by train to "work camps," which, in reality, were transit stations on the way to death camps in the east. Outraged, the people of Amsterdam called a general strike that shut down the city for two days...but the Nazis responded with even harsher laws.

Photos and artifacts bring to life the growing anxiety the Frank family endured. Jews were required to register with the police and wear a yellow-star patch. A map made in spring 1941 shows where Jews lived; each dot represents 10 Jews. School photos from December 1941 show Anne and Margot after they were forced to go to an all-Jewish school, leaving their Christian friends behind.

▶ *Go upstairs to the...*

Second Floor Storeroom

Think about the circumstances that forced the Franks to move in here.

In July 1942, Margot got her call-up notice for a "work-force project." Otto could see where this was headed. He handed over the keys to the business to his "Aryan" colleagues, sent a final postcard to relatives, gave the family cat to a neighbor, spread rumors that they were fleeing to Switzerland, and prepared his family to "dive under" (*onderduik,* as it was called) into hiding.

Photos put faces on the brave people who kept Otto's business running while the Frank family hid in the back of the building. Johannes Kleiman helped Otto set up the annex hiding place. During the Nazi occupation, Miep Gies, Otto's secretary, brought food to the Frank family every few days, while bookkeeper Victor Kugler cheered up Anne with the latest movie magazines.

Videos show interviews with Otto, Miep, and Victor from the 1960s and '70s, describing how they organized the concealment, got supplies, and set up the Secret Annex.

▸ *At the back of the second-floor storeroom is the clever hidden passageway into the Secret Annex.*

Secret Annex

The Secret Annex hid eight people in a tiny apartment smaller than 1,000 square feet. First were the Frank family—Otto and Edith and their daughters, 13-year-old Anne and 16-year-old Margot. A week later, they were joined by the Van Pels (called the "Van Daans" in her diary), with their teenage son, Peter. A few months later, Fritz Pfeffer (called "Mr. Dussel" in the diary) was invited in.

Though its furniture was ransacked during the arrest, the rooms of the annex remained virtually untouched, and we see them today much as they were.

Bookcase Entrance

On a rainy Monday morning, July 6, 1942, the Frank family—wearing extra clothes to avoid carrying suspicious suitcases—breathed their last fresh air, took a long look at the Prinsengracht canal, and disappeared into the back part of the building, where they spent the next two years. Victor Kugler concealed the entrance to the annex with this swinging bookcase, stacked with business files.

Though not exactly a secret (since it's hard to hide an entire building), the annex was a typical back-house (*achterhuis*), a common feature in Amsterdam buildings, and the Nazis had no reason to suspect anything on the premises of the legitimate Opekta business.

▸ *Pass through the bookcase entrance into...*

Otto, Edith, and Margot's Room

The family carried on life as usual. Edith read from a **prayer book** in their native German, Otto read Dickens' ***Sketches by Boz,*** and the children continued their studies, with Margot taking **Latin lessons** by correspondence course. They avidly followed the course of the war through radio broadcasts and news from their helpers. As the tides of war slowly turned and it appeared they might one day be saved from the Nazis, Otto tracked the Allied advance with colored pushpins on a **map** of Normandy.

The room is very small, even without the furniture. Imagine yourself and two fellow tourists confined here for two years.

Pencil lines on the wall track Margot's and Anne's heights, marking the point at which these growing lives were cut short.

Anne Frank's Room

Pan the room clockwise to see some of the young girl's idols in photos and clippings she pasted there herself: American stars Robert Stack and Deanna Durbin from the Cinderella-story film First Love, the future Queen Elizabeth II as a child, matinee idol Rudy Vallee, figure-skating actress Sonja Henie, and, on the other wall, actress Greta Garbo, actor Ray Milland, Renaissance man Leonardo da Vinci, and actress Ginger Rogers. Photos of flowers and landscapes gave Anne a window on the outside world she was forbidden to see.

Out the window (which had to be blacked out) is the back courtyard, which had a chestnut tree and a few buildings. (In 2010, the tree, which Anne had greatly enjoyed, toppled in a storm.) These things, along with the Westerkerk bell chiming every 15 minutes, represented the borders of Anne's "outside world." Imagine Anne sitting here at a small desk, writing in her diary.

In November 1942, the Franks invited a Jewish neighbor to join them, and Anne was forced to share the tiny room with Fritz Pfeffer, a middle-aged dentist.

Bathroom

The eight inhabitants shared this bathroom. During the day, they didn't dare flush the toilet.

▶ *Ascend the steep staircase—silently—to the...*

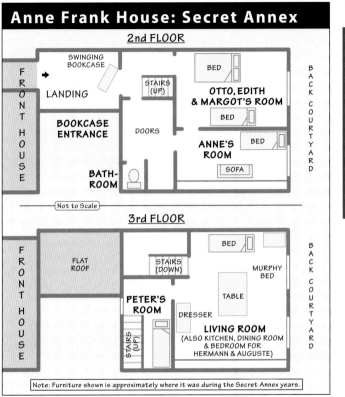

Anne Frank House: Secret Annex

2nd FLOOR

SWINGING BOOKCASE

FRONT HOUSE

LANDING

BOOKCASE ENTRANCE

BATH-ROOM

STAIRS (UP)

DOORS

BED

BED

OTTO, EDITH & MARGOT'S ROOM

BED

ANNE'S ROOM

SOFA

BACK COURTYARD

Not to Scale

3rd FLOOR

FRONT HOUSE

FLAT ROOF

STAIRS (DOWN)

PETER'S ROOM

DRESSER

STAIRS (UP)

BED

MURPHY BED

TABLE

LIVING ROOM
(ALSO KITCHEN, DINING ROOM & BEDROOM FOR HERMANN & AUGUSTE)

BACK COURTYARD

Note: Furniture shown is approximately where it was during the Secret Annex years.

Common Living Room

This was the kitchen (note the remains of the stove and sink) and dining room. Otto Frank was well off, and early on, the annex was well stocked with food. Miep Gies would dutifully take their shopping list, buy food for her "family" of eight, and secretly lug it up to them. Buying such large quantities in a coupon-rationed economy was highly suspect, but she knew a sympathetic grocer (a block away on Leliegracht) who was part of a ring of Amsterdammers risking their lives to help the Jews.

Life in the Annex

By day, it's enforced silence, so no one can hear them in the offices. They whisper, tiptoe, and step around squeaky places in the floor. The windows are blacked out, so they can't even look outside. They read or study, and Anne writes in her diary.

At night and on weekends, when the offices close, one or two might sneak downstairs to listen to Winston Churchill's BBC broadcasts on the office radio. Everyone's spirits rise and sink with news of Allied victories and setbacks.

Anne's diaries make clear the tensions, petty quarrels, and domestic politics of eight people living under intense pressure. Mr. Van Pels annoys Anne, but he gets along well with Margot. Anne never gets used to Mr. Pfeffer, who is literally invading her space. Most troublesome of all, pubescent Anne often strikes sparks with her mom. (Anne's angriest comments about her mother were deleted from early editions of the published diary.)

Despite their hardships, the group feels guilty: They have shelter, while so many other Jews are being rounded up and sent off. As the war progresses, they endure long nights when the house shakes from Allied air raids, and Anne cuddles up in her dad's bed.

Boredom tinged with fear—the existentialist hell of living in hiding is captured so well in Anne's journal.

The **menu** for a special dinner lists soup, roast beef, salad, potatoes, rice, dessert, and coffee. Later, as war and German restrictions plunged Holland into poverty and famine, they survived on canned foods and dried kidney beans.

The inhabitants spent their days reading and studying in this room. At night, it became sleeping quarters for Hermann and Auguste van Pels.

Peter van Pels' Room

On Peter's 16th birthday, he got a Monopoly-like board game called "The Broker" as a present. Initially, Anne was cool toward Peter, but after two years together, a courtship developed, and their flirtation culminated in a kiss.

The **staircase** (no visitor access) leads up to where the inhabitants stored their food. Anne loved to steal away here for a bit of privacy. At night they'd open a hatch to let in fresh air.

One hot August day, Otto was in this room helping Peter learn English, when they looked up to see a man with a gun. The hiding was over.

▸ *From here we leave the Secret Annex, returning to the Opekta storeroom and offices in the front house. As you work your way downstairs, you'll see a number of exhibits on the aftermath of this story.*

Aftermath

Arrest, Deportation, and Auschwitz Exhibits

On August 4, 1944, a German policeman accompanied by three Dutch Nazis pulled up in a car, politely entered the Opekta office, and went straight to the bookcase entrance. No one knows who tipped them off. The police gave the surprised hiders time to pack. They demanded their valuables and stuffed them into Anne's briefcase...after dumping her diaries onto the floor.

Taken in a van to Gestapo headquarters, the eight were processed in an efficient, bureaucratic manner, then placed on a train to Westerbork, a concentration camp northeast of the city. You'll see the **transport list,** which includes "Anneliese Frank," and their 3-by-5-inch **registration cards.**

From there they were locked in a car on a normal passenger train and sent to Auschwitz, a Nazi extermination camp in Poland. On the platform at Auschwitz, they were "forcibly separated from each other" (as Otto later reported) and sent to different camps. Anne and Margot were sent to Bergen-Belsen.

If it's playing, don't miss the **video** of one of Anne's former neighbors, Hannah Goslar, who ended up at Bergen-Belsen with Anne. In English she describes their reunion as they talked through a barbed-wire fence shortly before Anne died. She says of Anne, "She didn't have any more tears."

Anne and Margot both died of typhus in March 1945, only weeks before the camp was liberated. The other Secret Annex residents—except Otto—were gassed or died of disease.

The Franks' story was that of Holland's Jews. The seven who died were among the more than 100,000 Dutch Jews killed during the war years. (Before the war, 140,000 Jews lived in the Netherlands.) Of Anne's school class of 87 Jews, only 20 survived.

▶ *The next room is devoted to…*

The Diaries

Anne wrote three different diaries. (You may see one, two, or all three of them, as well as individual pages.) She received the first diary (with a red-plaid binding) as a birthday present when she turned 13, shortly before the family went into hiding. The other two were written in school-exercise books. Anne wrote the diaries in the form of a letter to an imaginary friend named Kitty.

As she wrote more and more, Anne began to recognize the uniqueness of her situation. You may see some loose-leaf pages on which she reworked parts of her diary. You may also see a book of Anne's short stories and a notebook in which she compiled "beautiful sentences" from books she'd read.

When the diaries were published, the book quickly became a best-seller. *De Achterhuis,* "The Back House" in Dutch, soon became *The Diary of a Young Girl* in English (1952), followed by translations in many other languages. The book became a popular play, *The Diary of Anne Frank,* and then a Hollywood movie.

▶ *Downstairs you come to…*

The Otto Frank Room

After the war, Otto returned to Amsterdam. The displayed newspaper notice he placed in August 1945 seeking information about his daughters is heartbreaking. In November of that year he received confirmation that they had died in Bergen-Belsen.

Miep Gies gave him Anne's diaries, which she had found on the floor of the annex after the arrest. Listen to a 1967 **video,** in which Anne's father talks about his reaction as he read the diaries. He was struck by the enormous power of Anne's ideas and emotions—a secret world he'd never known inside his daughter. Determined to make her writings available to a wider audience, he set about contacting publishers (you may see his letters or notebooks or early typed-up drafts of the diaries). In 1947, the diaries were first published in Dutch as *De Achterhuis*.

▶ *Continue downstairs to the ground-floor exhibits.*

Anne's Legacy

These displays (which change often) capture the Anne Frank legacy.

You may see video interviews of people who knew Anne, such as childhood friends or Miep Gies (who passed away in 2010 at the age of 100). You may see memorabilia of the Franks and their friends (or even the Oscar statuette won by Shelley Winters for the 1959 movie). Scale models of the annex with furniture created in the early 1960s were based on details from Otto and used as a source for multiple film sets. You may learn about Otto's struggles to save the house from demolition and turn it into a museum.

Otto wanted the Anne Frank House to be, in his words, "more than a museum." Its displays do not try to sum up "the moral" of the story. Instead, they recognize that World War II presented many gray areas and ethical dilemmas, and different people had different responses. The point? To keep visitors from leaving the museum with pat feelings of easy moral clarity.

The Anne Frank Foundation is obviously concerned that we learn from Europe's Nazi nightmare. The thinking that made the Holocaust possible still survives. Even today, some groups promote the notion that the Holocaust never occurred and contend that stories like Anne Frank's are only a hoax. It was Otto Frank's dream that visitors come away from the Anne Frank House with hope for a better world. He wrote: "The task that Anne entrusted to me continually gives me new strength to strive for reconciliation and for human rights all over the world."

Sights

Dynamic Amsterdam, laced with shimmering canals and lined with golden-age architecture, boasts magnificent museums, from the venerable Rijksmuseum (with Dutch Masters) to Van Gogh's starry collection to the thought-provoking Anne Frank House. The city has perhaps more small specialty museums than any other city its size. From houseboats to sex, from marijuana to the Dutch resistance, you can find a museum to suit your interests.

The following sights are arranged by neighborhood for handy sightseeing. When you see a 📖 in a listing, it means the sight is covered in much more depth in one of the self-guided walks or tours in this book. A 🎧 means the walk or tour is available as a free audio tour (see page 12).

Remember that, though the city has several must-see museums, its best attraction is its own carefree ambience.

Amsterdam Sights

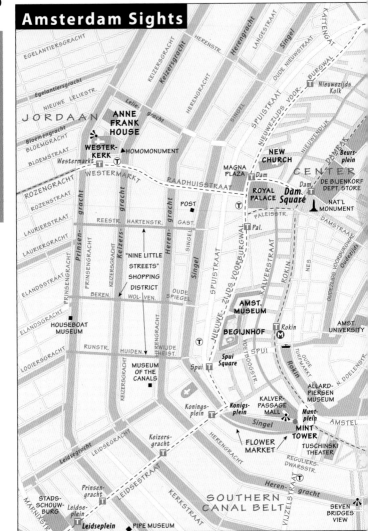

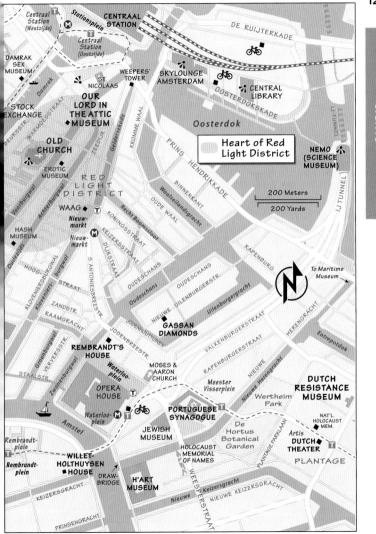

CENTRAAL STATION

Centraal Station (Westzijde)

Centraal Station (Oostzijde)

Stationsplein

DE RUIJTERKADE

DAMRAK SEX MUSEUM

Damrak

WEEPERS' TOWER

SKYLOUNGE AMSTERDAM

CENTRAL LIBRARY

OOSTERDOKSKADE

ST. NICOLAAS

STOCK EXCHANGE

BEURSSTR.

WARMOESSTRAAT

Voorburgwal

OUR LORD IN THE ATTIC MUSEUM

ZEEDIJK

KROMME WAAL

GELDERSKADE

Oosterdok

PRINS HENDRIKKADE

NEMO (SCIENCE MUSEUM)

Heart of Red Light District

IJ TUNNEL

OLD CHURCH

EROTIC MUSEUM

RED LIGHT DISTRICT

Achterburgwal

Oudezijds

HASH MUSEUM

WAAG

Nieuwmarkt

Nieuwmarkt

KONINGSSTRAAT

RECHT BOOMSSLOOT

OUDE WAAL

Waalseilandgracht

BINNENKANT

200 Meters

200 Yards

HOOG-

KLOVENIERSBURGWAL

Kloveniers-burgwal

STRAAT

ZANDSTR.

RAAMGRACHT

KEIZERSSTRAAT

DIJKSTRAAT

S. ANTONIESBREESTR.

OUDESCHANS

NIEUWE UILENBURGERSTR.

Oudeschans

JODENBREESTR.

JODENHOUTTUINEN

GASSAN DIAMONDS

UILENBURGERGRACHT

RAPENBURG

To Maritime Museum

VALKENBURGERSTRAAT

HERENGRACHT

Entrepotdok

Entrepotdok

Groenburgwal

VERVERSSTR.

Zwanenburgwal

STAALSTR.

REMBRANDT'S HOUSE

Waterloo-plein

MOSES & AARON CHURCH

RAPENBURGERSTRAAT

NIEUWE

DUTCH RESISTANCE MUSEUM

OPERA HOUSE

Waterloo-plein

Amstel

Rembrandt-plein

Rembrandt-plein

PORTUGUESE SYNAGOGUE

JEWISH MUSEUM

Meester Visserplein

Nieuwe Herengracht

Wertheim Park

NAT'L. HOLOCAUST MEM.

De Hortus Botanical Garden

Artis DUTCH THEATER

PLANTAGE

PLANTAGE PARKLAAN

WILLET-HOLTHUYSEN HOUSE

DRAW-BRIDGE

H'ART MUSEUM

HOLOCAUST MEMORIAL OF NAMES

KEIZERSGRACHT

Nieuwe Keizersgracht

NIEUWE KEIZERSGRACHT

WEESPERSTRAAT

PRINSENGRACHT

Advance Tickets and Sightseeing Passes

Buy timed-entry tickets online in advance for Amsterdam's three most popular museums: the **Anne Frank House** (tickets released six weeks in advance every Tuesday), **Van Gogh Museum** (reserve at least a week in advance), and **Rijksmuseum.** In peak season, it's also smart to buy tickets online in advance for the **Stedelijk Museum.**

Always book directly on the sight's official website. You'll select your preferred date and entry time (usually with a 30-minute window to enter), then make the purchase with your credit card. Once you've booked, you'll receive an email—usually with a QR code—that acts as your digital ticket. When you get to the sight at your designated time, pull up the digital ticket on your phone, scan it, and walk right in.

You'll need to book a timed entry even if you're buying a sightseeing pass; you can make a reservation online before you receive your pass, but you'll need to present the pass with your reservation at the sight.

I Amsterdam City Card: If you'll use public transportation and plan to pack in a lot of sights, this pass can save you some cash. It provides free or discounted entry to many sights in and around Amsterdam (but not the Anne Frank House or Van Gogh Museum). It also includes a canal cruise, bike rental, and transit pass (€65/24

Buy tickets online in advance to guarantee entry.

hours, €90/48 hours, €110/72 hours, buy at the I Amsterdam store in Centraal station or download the app to purchase; for details see www.iamsterdamcard.com).

Museumkaart: This sightseeing pass might save you a little money, but you can only use it at five sights—of your choosing—out of the 450 sights it covers (€65, valid 31 days, full details and list of covered sights at www.museumkaart.nl).

Southwest Amsterdam

▲Museumplein

Bordered by the Rijks, Van Gogh, and Stedelijk museums, and the Concertgebouw (classical music hall), this park-like square is interesting even to art haters. Amsterdam's best acoustics are found underneath the Rijksmuseum, where street musicians perform everything from chamber music to Mongolian throat singing. Locals enjoy a park bench or a coffee at the Cobra Café (playground nearby). The gardens (*tuinen*) by the Rijksmuseum are free to enter and a peaceful place to enjoy a coffee.

Nearby is **Coster Diamonds,** a handy place to see a diamond-cutting and -polishing demo (free, frequent, and interesting 30-minute tours followed by sales pitch, daily 9:00-17:00, Paulus Potterstraat 2, +31 20 305 5555, https://royalcoster.com). The end of the tour leads you straight into their Diamond Múseum, which is worthwhile only for those who feel the need to see even more diamonds (€11, daily 9:00-17:00, +31 20 305 5300, www.diamondmuseum.com).

▲▲▲Rijksmuseum

Built to house the nation's great art, the Rijksmuseum (RIKES-moo-zay-oom) owns several thousand paintings, including an incomparable collection of 17th-century Dutch Masters: Rembrandt, Vermeer, Hals, and Steen. Its vast collection also includes interesting artifacts—such as furniture—that help bring the golden age to life.

📖 See the Rijksmuseum Tour chapter.

▲▲▲Van Gogh Museum

Near the Rijksmuseum, this remarkable museum features works by the troubled Dutch artist whose art seemed to mirror his life. Highlights include *Sunflowers, The Bedroom, The Potato Eaters,* and many brooding self-portraits.

📖 See the Van Gogh Museum Tour chapter.

Southwest Amsterdam

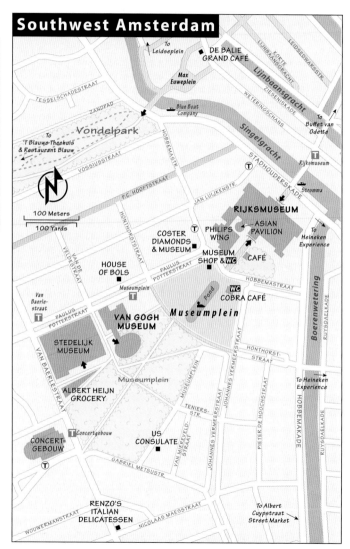

Planning a Three-Museum Day

To see the art at the Rijksmuseum, Van Gogh Museum, and Stedelijk Museum in a single day, there are two good strategies to keep in mind when buying timed-entry tickets in advance.

One approach is to see the museums chronologically, in historical order: First, take in the Old Masters at the Rijks, then Impressionism at the Van Gogh, and finish with modern art at the Stedelijk.

But if you're in town during the busy season, you can avoid crowds by following this plan: See the Van Gogh Museum right when it opens at 9:00, then visit the less-congested Stedelijk. From there, you could have lunch and take in some extra nearby sights—such as Coster Diamonds and the House of Bols. Finally, hit the Rijksmuseum after 14:00, when crowds there begin to subside.

▲▲Stedelijk Museum

The Netherlands' top modern-art museum is filled with a permanent collection of 20th-century classics as well as far-out, refreshing, cutting-edge temporary exhibits. You'll run across some famous works by Picasso, Chagall, and many more, but be sure to also pay special attention to the many Dutch artists who helped to create modern art.

▶ €20, daily 10:00-18:00, top-notch gift shop, Museumplein 10, +31 20 573 2911, www.stedelijk.nl.

House of Bols: Cocktail & Genever Experience

This "experience" is a self-guided walk through what is essentially an ad for Holland's leading distillery, culminating in a chance to taste local gins.

▶ €16; daily 13:00-18:30, Fri-Sat until 21:00, last entry one hour before closing; must be 18, Paulus Potterstraat 14, www.houseofbols.com.

Heineken Experience

This famous brewery, having moved its operations to the suburbs, has converted its old headquarters into a slick-yet-cheesy beerfest—complete with a video-surround beer-making simulation in which visitors are brewed and bottled. It can be a fun trip—like visiting a beer lover's amusement park—if you can ignore the fact that you're essentially paying for 90 minutes of advertising.

The Stedelijk has wild modern art.

Museumplein—a people-friendly park

▶ *€21 for timed-entry ticket—buy online or at kiosk in lobby, includes two drinks; daily 10:30-19:30, Fri-Sun until 21:00, longer hours July-Aug, last entry 2 hours before closing; tram #24 to Marie Heinekenplein, Stadhouderskade 78; +31 20 721 5300, www.heinekenexperience.com.*

▲Vondelpark

This huge, lively city park is popular with the Dutch—families with little kids, romantic couples, strolling seniors, and hipsters sharing blankets and beers. It's a favored venue for free summer concerts. On a sunny afternoon, it's a hedonistic scene that seems to say, "Parents...relax."

Southern Canal Belt

The ring of canals south of the historic core hosts a few small museums and some of the city's best nightlife.

▲Leidseplein

Brimming with cafés, this people-watching mecca is an impromptu stage for street artists, accordionists, jugglers, and unicyclists. It's particularly bustling on sunny afternoons. After dark, it's a vibrant tourists' nightclub center. Stroll nearby Lange Leidsedwarsstraat (one block north) for a taste-bud tour of multicultural eateries, from Greek to Indonesian.

Amsterdam Pipe Museum

This small and unusual-yet-classy museum holds 300 years of pipes in a 17th-century canal house. (It's almost worth the admission price just to see the inside of one of these elegant homes.) You enter through the street-level shop, which is almost interesting enough to be a museum itself.

Heineken brewery—a frothy "experience"

Vondelpark—paths, greenery, happy locals

▶ *€12.50, Mon-Sat 12:00-18:00, closed Sun, +31 20 421 1779, just off Leidsestraat at Prinsengracht 488, www.pijpenkabinet.nl.*

Rembrandtplein and Tuschinski Theater

One of the city's premier nightlife spots is the leafy Rembrandtplein (and the adjoining Thorbeckeplein). Several late-night dance clubs keep the area lively into the wee hours. Utrechtsestraat is lined with upscale shops and restaurants. The nearby **Tuschinski Theater,** a movie palace from the 1920s (a half-block from Rembrandtplein down Reguliersbreestraat), glitters inside and out. The exterior is an interesting hybrid of styles, forcing the round peg of Art Nouveau into the square hole of Art Deco. Inside (lobby is free), the sumptuous decor features fancy carpets, slinky fixtures, and semi-abstract designs. To see much more of the interior, take one of their excellent self-guided audio tours.

▶ *€10 for half-hour tour, daily 9:30-11:00—get there by 10:00; Reguliersbreestraat 26.*

▲Willet-Holthuysen House (Huis Willet-Holthuisen)

This 1687 townhouse is a must for devotees of Hummel-topped sugar bowls and Louis XVI-style wainscoting. For others, it's a pleasant look inside a typical (rich) home with much of the original furniture and decor. Forget the history and just browse through a dozen rooms of beautiful saccharine objects from the 19th century.

▶ *€12.50, includes audioguide, daily 10:00-17:00; tram #4 or #14 to Rembrandtplein, Herengracht 605, +31 20 523 1822, www.willetholthuysen.nl.*

The Dutch Made Holland

The word Nederland means "lowland." ("Holland" is just a nickname; North and South Holland are two of the country's 12 provinces.) The country occupies the delta near the mouth of three of Europe's large rivers, including the Rhine. In medieval times, inhabitants built a system of earthen dikes to protect their land from flooding caused by tides and storm surges. Much of the land of the Netherlands was reclaimed from the sea, rivers, and lakes.

Though less than 10 percent of the Dutch labor force is in agriculture, more than 50 percent of the land is cultivated: If you venture outside of Amsterdam, you'll travel through vast fields. Several Dutch icons originated directly from the country's unique landscape: Windmills and canals drained the land. Wooden shoes (klompen) allowed farmers to walk across soggy fields. (The shoes also float—making them easy to find should they come off in high water.) Tulips and other flowers grew well in the sandy soil near dunes. All this tinkering with nature prompted a popular local saying: "God made the Earth, but the Dutch made Holland."

West Amsterdam

The mostly residential neighborhood around many of these sights is described in the 📖 Jordaan Walk chapter and 🎧 audio tour.

▲▲▲ Anne Frank House

Thirteen-year-old Anne and her family spent two years hiding in the back rooms of this townhouse during the Nazi occupation of World War II. The thoughtfully designed exhibit offers thorough coverage of the Frank family, the diary, the stories of others who hid, and the Holocaust.

📖 See the Anne Frank House Tour chapter.

Houseboat Museum (Woonbootmuseum)

In the 1930s, modern cargo ships came into widespread use—making small, sail-powered cargo boats obsolete. In danger of extinction, these little vessels found new life as houseboats lining the canals of Amsterdam. Today, 2,500 such boats—their cargo holds turned into classy, comfortable living rooms—are called home. For a peek into this gezellig (cozy) world, visit this tiny museum aboard the *Hendrika*

Maria, a former cargo ship built in 1914. Captain Vincent enjoys showing visitors around his houseboat, which feels lived-in because, until 1997, it was.

▶ *€4.50; daily 10:00-17:00 except closed Mon Sept-June; on Prinsengracht, opposite #296 facing Elandsgracht, +31 20 427 0750, www.houseboatmuseum.nl.*

Westerkerk

Located near the Anne Frank House, this landmark Protestant church has an appropriately barren interior, Rembrandt's body buried somewhere under the pews, and Amsterdam's tallest steeple with a grand view. The Westerkerk tower is climbable only with a guided tour (185 steps, currently closed for restoration).

▶ *Free, donation requested; generally Mon-Sat 11:00-15:00, closed Sun; Prinsengracht 281, +31 20 624 7766, www.westerkerk.nl.*

Museum of the Canals (Grachtenmuseum)

Located in what was once a grand 17th-century canal house, this museum tells the story of Amsterdam's evolution of canals, streets, and buildings, creatively using video projections and 3-D displays.

▶ *€15, includes audioguide, Tue-Sun 10:00-17:00, closed Mon, Herrengracht 386, +31 20 4211 656, www.hetgrachtenhuis.nl.*

Central Amsterdam, near Dam Square

Connect the following sights with my 📖 Amsterdam City Walk chapter and 🎧 audio tour.

▲Royal Palace (Koninklijk Huis)

This palace was built as a lavish City Hall (1648-1655), when Holland

Anne Frank House—now a museum

Houseboat Museum with Captain Vincent

was a proud new republic and Amsterdam was the richest city on the planet—awash in profit from trade. The building became a "Royal Palace" when Napoleon installed his brother Louis as king (1806). After Napoleon's fall, it continued as a royal residence for the Dutch royal family, the House of Orange. Today, it's one of King Willem-Alexander's official residences. About 20 lavishly decorated rooms are open to the public.

The highlight is the vast, white **Citizens' Hall**—120 feet by 60 feet by 90 feet, and lit by eight big chandeliers. At the far end, a statue of Atlas holds the globe of the world, and the ceiling painting shows Lady Amsterdam triumphant amid the clouds of heaven. On the floor, inlaid maps show the known world circa 1750 (back when the West Coast of the US was still being explored). The hall is used today to host foreign dignitaries and for royal family wedding receptions.

You'll also see the room where Louis Bonaparte's throne once sat (in front of the fireplace), a room of impressive Empire Style furniture (high-polished wood with Neoclassical motifs), and the childhood bedroom of former Queen Beatrix. The palace's rich chandeliers, paintings, statues, and furniture reflect Amsterdam's historic status as the center of global trade.

▶ *€12.50, includes good multimedia guide, daily 10:00-17:00 but hours can vary for official ceremonies—check website, +31 20 522 6161, www. paleisamsterdam.nl.*

New Church (Nieuwe Kerk)

Barely newer than the Red Light District's "Old" Church, this 15th-century sanctuary has an intentionally spare interior, its decoration removed by 16th-century iconoclastic Protestants seeking to unclutter their communion with God. This is where many Dutch royal weddings and all inaugurations take place.

▶ *Interior with special exhibits-€9-16, daily 10:00-18:00, audioguide-€4 or free depending on exhibit, on Dam Square, +31 20 626 8168, www. nieuwekerk.nl.*

▲▲Amsterdam Museum

Amsterdam's city history museum is closed while its permanent building is undergoing renovation until 2025; a temporary exhibit may be on display at the H'ART Museum (described later in this chapter). Also closed is the Amsterdam Gallery (formerly known as the "Civic

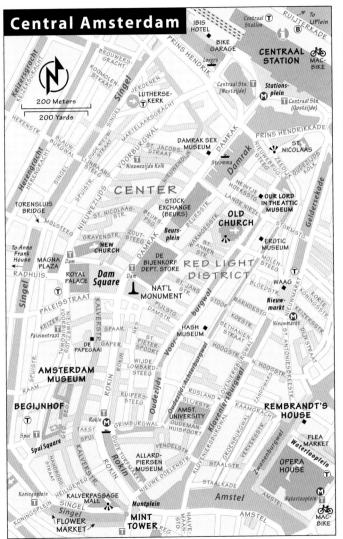

Central Amsterdam

200 Meters
200 Yards

Keizersgracht
KEIZERSGRACHT

Singel

BROUWERS-
GRACHT

IBIS
HOTEL

BIKE
GARAGE

PRINS HENDRIK.

Centraal
Station

To IJPlein
RUIJTERKADE

B

CENTRAAL
STATION

MAC-
BIKE

Lovers

Centraal Stn.
(Westzijde)

Stations-
plein

Centraal Stn.
(Oostzijde)

Herengracht
HERENGRACHT

BLAUW-
BURGWAL

ROOMOLEN-
STRAAT

JEROENEN

LUTHERSE-
KERK

JEROENEN

MARTELAARSGRACHT

PRINS HENDRIKKADE

ST. NICOLAAS

DAMRAK SEX
MUSEUM

ST. JACOBS-
STRAAT

OUDE NIEUW-
STRAAT

LIJNBAANS-
STEEG

SPUISTR.

VOORBURGWAL

Nieuwezijds Kolk

NIEUWENDIJK

Stromma

DAMRAK

NIEUWEBRUG-
STEEG

OUDEZIJDS
KOLK

Heintje
HOEKSTG.

Lange Niezel

OUR LORD
IN THE ATTIC
MUSEUM

HERENSTR.

HEKENGRACHT

CENTER

STOCK
EXCHANGE
(BEURS)

ST. NICOLAAS-
STR.

BEURSSTR.

BEURS-
PSG.

WARMOESSTR.

OLD
CHURCH

Gelderselkade

STORMSTG.

EROTIC
MUSEUM

MOLEN-
STEEG

TORENSLUIS
BRIDGE

MOLSTEEG

GRAVENSTR.

ZOUT-
STEEG

Beurs-
plein

ST.
ANNEN
STR.

ST.
WANNEN
STR.

To Anne
Frank
House

MAGNA
PLAZA

NEW
CHURCH

Dam

DAMRAK

RADHUIS.

ROYAL
PALACE

Dam Square

Dam

DE
BIJENKORF
DEPT. STORE

RED LIGHT
DISTRICT

WAAG

BLOEDSTR.

Nieuw-
markt

KORTE
KONINGSSTR.

NIEUWMARKT

ST. ANTONIES-
BREESTR.

Singel

PALEISSTRAAT

NAT'L
MONUMENT

ST. JANS-
BURGWAL

ST.
PULSTG.

STOOF

BARNDESTR.

KOESTR.

Nieuwmarkt

KEIZER-
NIEUWEZIJDS
VOORBURGWAL

SPAAR

NES

DAMSTR.

HASH
MUSEUM

BETHANIEN-
STRAAT

Paleisstraat

DE
PAPEGAAI

GAPER.

ST.
PIETER-
SPOORT

HOOGSTR.

N. HOOGSTR.

KLOVENIERSBURGWAL

ZANDSTR.

AMSTERDAM
MUSEUM

ROKIN

WIJDE
LOMBARD-
STEEG

Voor.

burgwal

KLOVENIER

RAAM

KUIPERS-
STEEG

OUDEZIJDS

RUSLAND

RAAMGRACHT

REMBRANDT'S
HOUSE

BEGIJNHOF

Rokin

SLIJKSTR.

GRIMBURGWAL

AMST.
UNIVERSITY

OUDEMAN-
HUISPOORT

OUDEZIJDS-ACHTERBURGWAL

GROENBURGWAL

FLEA
MARKET

Waterlooplein

Spui

Spui Square

TAKST

SPUI

OUDE TURFMARKT

VENDELSTR.

STAALSTR.

VERVERSSTR.

OPERA
HOUSE

KALVERSTR.

HANDBOG-
STR.

HEILIGEWEG

GED. BEG.

ALLARD-
PIERSEN
MUSEUM

NIEUWE DOELENSTR.

STAALKADE

Zwanenburgwal

Amstel

Waterlooplein

MAC-
BIKE

Koningsplein

KALVERPASSAGE
MALL

SINGEL

Muntplein

MINT
TOWER

HALVE-
MAAN-
STG.

REG.

AMSTEL

Singel

KONINGSPLEIN

FLOWER
MARKET

AMSTEL

Guards Gallery"), the museum's public corridor lined with group portraits of Amsterdam citizens from the golden age to now.

▲Begijnhof

Stepping into this tiny, idyllic courtyard in the city center, you escape into the charm of old Amsterdam. Notice house #34, a 500-year-old wooden structure (rare, since repeated fires taught city fathers a trick called brick).

See page 28 of the Amsterdam City Walk chapter.

Red Light District

Between Damrak and Nieuwmarkt, this neighborhood is one of Amsterdam's oldest and has hosted prostitutes since 1200.

▲▲Red Light District Walk

Europe's most popular ladies of the night tease and tempt here, as they have for centuries, in about 200 display-case windows around Oudezijds Achterburgwal and Oudezijds Voorburgwal, surrounding the Old Church (Oude Kerk). Drunks and druggies make the streets uncomfortable late at night, but it's a fascinating walk earlier in the evening.

📖 See the Red Light District Walk chapter.

Sex Museums

Amsterdam has three sex museums. While visiting one can be called sightseeing, visiting more than that is harder to explain.

The cheapest and most interesting is the **Damrak Sex Museum,** which tells the story of pornography from Roman times through 1960. Sexual deviations from all over the world are revealed, including early French pornographic photos; memorabilia from Europe, India, and Asia; a Marilyn Monroe tribute; and some S&M displays (€5, daily 10:00-18:00, Damrak 18, a block in front of Centraal station, +31 20 622 8376, www.sexmuseumamsterdam.nl).

The **Erotic Museum** in the Red Light District is five floors of uninspired paintings, videos, old photos, and sculpture (€7, daily 11:00-24:00, along the canal at Oudezijds Achterburgwal 54, +31 20 624 7303, www.erotisch-museum.nl).

Red Light Secrets Museum of Prostitution is a pricey look at the world's oldest profession. If you're wondering what it's like to sit in those red booths, watch the video taken from a sex worker's perspective as "johns" check you out (€14.50; Sun-Thu 11:00-22:00, Fri-Sat until 23:00; Oudezijds Achterburgwal 60, +31 20 846 7020, www.redlightsecrets.com).

▲▲Our Lord in the Attic Museum

For two centuries (1578-1795), Catholicism in Amsterdam was illegal but tolerated. When hard-line Protestants took power in 1578, Catholic churches were vandalized and shut down. The city's Catholics were forbidden to worship openly, so they gathered secretly to say Mass in homes and offices. In 1663, a wealthy merchant built Our Lord in the Attic (Ons' Lieve Heer op Solder), one of a handful of places in Amsterdam that served as a secret parish church until Catholics were once again allowed to worship in public.

The church was hidden within the businessman's own home. From the outside, it's a typical townhouse on a historic canal. But within lies a 150-seat, three-story church that's the size of a four-lane bowling alley. The museum's one-way route will take you through living spaces in the front of the townhouse, then the secret church, and finally the "back house" (achterhuis, a common feature in historic townhouses).

▶ *€15.50, includes audioguide; Mon-Fri 10:00-17:00, Sat until 18:00, Sun 13:00-18:00; near Centraal station at Oudezijds Voorburgwal 38, +31 20 624 6604, www.opsolder.nl.*

Northeast Amsterdam

NEMO (National Center for Science and Technology)

This kid-friendly science museum is a city landmark with its distinctive copper-green building, jutting up from the water like a sinking ship. Several floors feature permanent and rotating exhibits that allow kids (and adults) to explore topics such as light, sound, and gravity,

The historic Our Lord in the Attic house has… …a hidden Catholic church in the attic.

and play with bubbles or topple giant dominoes. Up top is a restaurant with a great city view.

▸ *€17.50, free for kids 3 and under, daily 10:00-17:30, closed Mon off-season, Oosterdok 2, +31 20 531 3233, www.nemosciencemuseum.nl. The roof terrace—open until 20:00 in the summer—is generally free.*

▲▲Netherlands Maritime Museum (Nederlands Scheepvaartmuseum)

This huge, slick, and kid-friendly collection of model ships, maps, and sea-battle paintings fills the 300-year-old Dutch Navy Arsenal. Given the Dutch seafaring heritage, this is an appropriately important and impressive place.

A highlight is the colorful replica ship *Amsterdam* moored behind the building. This was an 18th-century cargo ship for the Dutch East India Company. Wander the decks, then duck your head and check out the captain and surgeon's quarters. On the main deck, don a heavy virtual-reality headset and get a 15-minute shipside view of 17th-century Amsterdam (VR experience open 11:00-16:00). The ship is light on historical information, but it's still fun to get a hands-on look at old-time life at sea. The **Royal Barge**—in the building signed *De Koningssloep*—is no replica. Built for King William I in the early 19th century, this gaudy boat was a symbol of the House of Orange and is still seaworthy.

▸ *€17.50, €8.50 for kids 4-17, includes audioguide; credit card only, no cash; daily 10:00-17:00, closed Mon off-season; bus #22 or #43 from Centraal station to Kattenburgerplein 1, +31 20 523 2222, www. hetscheepvaartmuseum.com.*

North Amsterdam

EYE Filmmuseum

The most striking feature of the Amsterdam skyline is EYE, a film museum and cinema housed in an übersleek modern building immediately across the water from Centraal station. It is a complex of museum spaces and four theaters playing mostly art films plus a gallery of film posters, a shop, and a trendy terrace café with waterside seating.

▸ *General entry and main-floor exhibit are free, fee for films and exhibits; daily 10:00-19:00, cinemas open daily at 10:00 until last screening, +31 20 589 1400, www.eyefilm.nl.*

NEMO's ship-shape science museum

Go below decks at the Maritime Museum.

▲A'dam Tower

This mega entertainment complex offers 360-degree views of the city, with display panels pointing out landmarks and providing fun tidbits of history, along with a cocktail bar and plenty of comfy spots to relax and take in the view. For more thrills, try "Europe's highest swing" over the IJ or a virtual-reality rollercoaster ride over Amsterdam. There's also a revolving restaurant and a nightclub.

▶ *Observation deck-€16.50; swing or VR ride-€6, family and combo-tickets available; daily 10:00-22:00, last entry one hour before closing, Overhoeksplein 1, www.adamtoren.nl.*

Southeast Amsterdam

Waterlooplein Flea Market

For more than a hundred years, the Jewish Quarter flea market has raged daily except Sunday (at the Waterlooplein Metro station, behind Rembrandt's House). The long, narrow park is filled with stalls selling cheap clothes, hippie stuff, old records, and tourist knickknacks.

▲Rembrandt's House (Museum Het Rembrandthuis)

A middle-aged Rembrandt lived here from 1639 to 1658 after his wife's death, as his popularity and wealth dwindled down to obscurity and bankruptcy. The house is reconstructed and filled with period objects (not his actual belongings) that re-create what Rembrandt's bankruptcy inventory of 1656 said he owned. Imagine Rembrandt at work here in the well-lighted room where he created *The Night Watch, The Portrait of Maria Trip,* and numerous self-portraits (seen at the Rijksmuseum). You can attend an etching demonstration and ask the printer to explain the etching process. For the finale, enjoy several

Southeast Amsterdam

To Red Light District
N. HOOGSTR
Oude Schans
NIEUWE UILENBURGERGRACHT
Uilenburgergracht
Ullenburgerstraat
VALKENBURGERSTR
SCHIPPERSGRACHT
KADIJKSPLEIN
Entrepot Dok
ENTREPOTDOK
PLANTAGEKADE

REMBRANDT'S HOUSE
JODENBREESTR
GASSAN DIAMONDS
RAPEN-BURGERSTR
ANNE FRANKSTR
DUTCH RESISTANCE MUSEUM

VERVERSSTR
Waterlooplein
FLEA MARKET
MOSES & AARON CHURCH
PORTUGUESE SYNAGOGUE
Nieuwe Herengracht
Wertheim-park
PARKLAAN
H. POLAKLAAN

OPERA HOUSE
Meester Visserplein
Meester Visserplein
MUIDERSTR
NAT'L. HOLOCAUST MEM.
PARKLAAN

AMSTEL/Waterlooplein
NIEUWE AMSTELSTR
J. D. Meijerplein
PLANTAGE
De Hortus Botanical Garden
MIDDENLAAN
ARTIS ZOO

Amstel
JEWISH MUSEUM
DOCK WORKER STATUE
PLANTAGE
DUTCH THEATER
Artis/Plantage Kerklaan

BLAUW-BRUG
NIEUWE HERENGRACHT
HORTUSPLANTSOEN
WILLET-HOLTHUYSEN HOUSE
HOLOCAUST MEMORIAL OF NAMES
PLANTAGE MUIDERGRACHT
To Tropical Museum

DRAW-BRIDGE
H'ART MUSEUM
Nieuwe Keizersgracht
KEIZERSGRACHT
Plantage
Muidergracht

Herengracht
River
AMSTEL
Amstel
NIEUWE
WEESPERSTR
KERKSTRAAT

Keizersgracht
MAGERE BRIDGE
NIEUWE
Prinsengracht
NIEUWE PRINSENGRACHT

KERKSTRAAT
Nieuwe

200 Meters
200 Yards

rooms dedicated (generally) to original Rembrandt etchings. You're not likely to see a single Rembrandt painting in the whole house, but this interesting museum may make you come away wanting to know more about the man and his art.

▶ *€15, includes audioguide; Tue-Sun 10:00-18:00, closed Mon; etching and paint-making demonstrations almost hourly, Jodenbreestraat 4, +31 20 520 0400, www.rembrandthuis.nl.*

Gassan Diamonds

Many shops in this "city of diamonds" offer tours. Here you'll see experts behind magnifying glasses polishing the facets of precious diamonds, followed by a visit to an intimate sales room to see (and perhaps buy) a mighty shiny yet very tiny souvenir.

▶ *Free, daily 9:00-17:30, Nieuwe Uilenburgerstraat 173, +31 20 622 5333, www.gassan.com.*

H'ART Museum

After cutting ties with the Hermitage Museum in St. Petersburg in 2022, the Hermitage Amsterdam has rebranded itself as the H'ART Museum and will feature rotating exhibits from three famous museums: the Pompidou in Paris, the British Museum in London, and the Smithsonian American Art Museum of Washington, DC. Check their website to see what's on during your visit.

▶ *Ticket prices vary by exhibition; daily 10:00-17:00, mandatory free bag check, café, Amstel 51, +31 20 530 8755, www.hartmuseum.nl.*

De Hortus Botanical Garden

An oasis of tranquility within the city, this large park is one of the oldest botanical gardens in the world, from 1638. As Dutch sailors and botanists roamed the globe, they returned with medicinal herbs, cacti, tropical palms, and the first coffee plant in Europe.

▶ *€12, daily 10:00-17:00, tram #14 to Mr. Visserplein, Plantage Middenlaan 2A, +31 20 625 9021, www.dehortus.nl.*

▲Jewish Museum (Joods Museum) and Portuguese Synagogue

A single ticket admits you to these two sights, located a half-block apart. The Jewish Museum tells the story of the Netherlands' Jews through three centuries, serving as a good introduction to Judaism and Jewish customs and religious traditions. Nearby, the 17th-century Portuguese Synagogue is again in use by a Jewish congregation.

Start in the impressive Great Synagogue. Have a seat, surrounded by religious objects, and picture it during its prime (1671-1943). The vast hall would be full for a service—men downstairs, women above in

Rembrandt's House has a modern entrance.

Gassan's free diamond-polishing demo

the gallery. On the east wall (the symbolic direction of Jerusalem) is the ark—the alcove where they keep the scrolls of the Torah.

Displays (well described in English) around the room explain Jewish customs, from birth (circumcision) to puberty (the bar/bat mitzvah, celebrating the entry into adulthood) to Passover celebrations to marriage.

Next, head up the spiral staircase to the **women's gallery,** with exhibits tracing the history of Amsterdam's Jews from 1600 to 1900. Exhibits about Jews in the 20th century are housed in the former **New Synagogue.** Personal artifacts—chairs, clothes—tell the devastating story of the Holocaust in a very real way.

Finish your visit at the **Portuguese Synagogue.** Built in the 1670s, it was the world's largest. The building survived World War II, though most of its congregation did not.

▸ *€17; museum open daily 10:00-17:00; Portuguese Synagogue open Sun-Fri 10:00-17:00, closes earlier Dec-Jan and Fri off-season, closed Sat year-round; free audioguide, Jonas Daniel Meijerplein 2, +31 20 531 0310, www.jhm.nl.*

Holocaust Memorial of Names

Opened in 2021, this somber labyrinth of walls is designed in the shape of four Hebrew letters that mean "In memory of." It's made of 102,000 bricks, each with the name, date of birth, and age at death of a Dutch victim who was killed by the Nazis. To remember and give dignity to these people—as well as 220 Sinti and Roma victims—this memorial encourages visitors to walk thoughtfully through and ponder the humanity of this tragic time.

▸ *Free, daily 8:00-20:00, behind the Jewish Museum on Weesperstraat.*

▲Dutch Theater (Hollandsche Schouwburg), a.k.a. National Holocaust Memorial

Once a lively theater in the Jewish neighborhood and today a moving memorial, this building was used as an assembly hall for local Jews destined for Nazi concentration camps. As you enter, you'll see a wall covered with 6,700 family names, paying tribute to the more than 100,000 Jews deported and killed by the Nazis. Some 70,000 victims spent time here, awaiting transfer to concentration camps.

Upstairs is a dated-but-evocative history exhibit. There's a model of the ghetto and artifacts of the Nazi occupation—the roundups,

Holocaust Memorial of Names

Jews were imprisoned at the Dutch Theater.

mandatory ID cards, deportation papers, and film footage of Nazis loading Jews onto trains. Back downstairs in the ground-floor courtyard, notice the hopeful messages that visiting school groups attach to the wooden tulips.

▸ *Donation requested, free with Jewish Museum/Portuguese Synagogue ticket, daily 11:00-17:00, Plantage Middenlaan 24, +31 20 531 0380, www.hollandscheschouwburg.nl.*

▲▲Dutch Resistance Museum (Verzetsmuseum)

Bam—it's May 1940 and the Germans invade the Netherlands, destroy Rotterdam, drive Queen Wilhelmina into exile, and—in four short days of fighting—hammer home the message that resistance is futile.

This museum tells the rest of the story of how the Dutch survived under Nazi occupation from 1940 to 1945. They faced a timeless moral dilemma: Is it better to collaborate with a wicked system to effect small-scale change—or to resist outright, even if your efforts are doomed to fail? You'll learn why some chose the former, and others the latter.

You'll see propaganda movie clips, study forged ID cards under a magnifying glass, and read about ingenious and courageous efforts—big and small—to undermine the Nazi regime. Vandals turned Nazi V-for-Victory posters into W-for-Wilhelmina. Printers circulated underground newspapers. Farmers organized a milk strike. Ordinary citizens hid radios under floorboards and Jews inside closets. They suffered through the "Hunger Winter" of 1944 to 1945, during which 20,000 died. Finally, it was springtime, the Allies liberated the country, and Nazi helmets were turned into Dutch bedpans.

▸ *€12, includes audioguide; Mon-Fri 10:00-17:00, Sat-Sun from 11:00,* *mandatory free bag check, Plantage Kerklaan 61, +31 20 620 2535, www.verzetsmuseum.org.*

▲Tropical Museum (Tropenmuseum)

This imaginative museum focuses on Dutch colonialism in Suriname, the Caribbean, and Indonesia, exploring themes including expansion and trade, slavery and racism, and language and religion. Ride the elevator near the ticket desk to the top floor and circle your way down through this immense collection, opened in 1926 to give the Dutch people a peek at their vast colonial holdings.

▶ *€16; daily 10:00-17:00, closed Mon off-season; tram #14 to Linnaeusstraat 2, +31 20 568 8200, www.tropenmuseum.nl.*

Day Trips

The Netherlands' efficient train system turns much of the country into a feasible day trip. To get train schedules in advance, use the Dutch Rail website (www.ns.nl). Dutch train tickets are issued either electronically (with a QR code, through the NS app or website), or on paper "chipcards." It's best to download and use the **NS app.** When you buy a ticket through the app, you'll get an eticket (with a QR code to get through the turnstile). You can also buy tickets **online** at www. ns.nl. If you prefer to get tickets at the station, you can buy a **single ticket** at NS ticket machines or at a ticket desk.

▲▲Haarlem

A half-hour away by train, the town of Haarlem is an agreeable mix of quaintness, history, and contemporary Dutch life.

The center of town is the massive main church, the **Grote Kerk.** Inside the church is Holland's largest organ (5,000 pipes) plus quirky exhibits like a replica of Foucault's pendulum and a 400-year-old cannonball. A spacious square **(Grote Markt)** surrounds the church. Sip a coffee or beer at one of the cafés, and take in a view that's looked much the same for 700 years and has been captured in well-known paintings. The square hosts colorful market days on Monday (clothing) and Saturday (general).

Haarlem is the hometown of Frans Hals, and the **Frans Hals Museum** has the world's largest collection of his work. Stand eye-to-eye with life-size, lifelike, warts-and-all portraits of golden-age brewers, preachers, workers, bureaucrats, and housewives. Most impressive are Hals' monumental group portraits.

The **Teylers Museum,** the Netherlands' oldest, almost feels like a museum of a museum, with its well-preserved exhibits of fossils, minerals, and primitive electronic gadgetry.

The **Corrie ten Boom House** relates the inspirational story of a family that courageously hid Jews from the Nazis (visits by tour only, reservations smart). Finally (two blocks northeast of Grote Markt, off Lange Begijnestraat), you can stroll through quaint Haarlem's cozy little **Red Light District.**

▶ *Trains to Haarlem depart Amsterdam's Centraal station several times an hour. From Haarlem's train station, the town center, Grote Markt, is a 10-minute walk. There are two bike rental shops near the station (Green Bikes, www.greenbikes.nl, and Rent a Bike Haarlem, www. rentabikehaarlem.nl). Avoid Haarlem on Mondays when many sights are closed. Haarlem's friendly TI (VVV) is in the Town Hall building on Grote Markt (+31 23 531 7325, www.visithaarlem.com).*

▲Other Dutch Destinations

The charming, canal-laced town of **Delft** (hometown of Vermeer and blue-painted ceramics) and its neighbor city, **The Hague** (famous for

In Haarlem, the main church anchors a town that's both quaint and contemporary.

its Old Masters in the Maurithuis Gallery), make a rewarding day or two of sightseeing. **Arnhem** has the Netherlands Open-Air Museum and the Kröller-Müller Museum of Van Gogh paintings (in Hogue Veluwe National Park). The **Historic Triangle** offers a nostalgic loop trip on a steam train and boat. **Keukenhof's** flower garden is one of the world's best (open in spring only). College-town **Leiden** is the Netherlands' answer to Cambridge or Oxford, while mighty **Rotterdam**—which had its core and port bombed flat during World War II—now is Europe's busiest port with a gleaming modern skyline. Medieval Utrecht is known for its lively downtown core and Holland's top railway museum.

If you want more, there's also Edam (an adorable village), Alkmaar (best on Fridays in spring and summer for its cheese market), Aalsmeer (a bustling modern flower auction), Schokland (for a chance to walk on what was the bottom of the sea at this village/museum), and open-air folk museums at Enkhuizen and Zaanse Schans.

For more info on these places visit www.holland.com.

Activities

Amsterdam offers much more than famous museums. Consider a floating introduction to the city on a guided canal boat tour (some people prefer to cruise at night, when Amsterdam's bridges are illuminated). Explore Amsterdam's history, architecture, or food scene with a group or private walking tour. You can even pedal around the city with a guided bike tour, or rent a bike and follow my "do-it-yourself" tour.

To round out your experiences, go on a shopping blitz, spend an evening at the theater or a concert, roll with the locals on skate night, or—for those so inclined—enjoy an "herbal" experience at a traditional "coffeeshop" (a café selling marijuana).

TOURS

Traditional Canal Boat Tours

These long, low, tourist-laden boats leave continually from several docks around town for a relaxing—if uninspiring—one-hour introduction to the city (with recorded headphone commentary), worth ▲▲. Select a boat tour based on your proximity to its starting point. The I Amsterdam City Card covers one cruise from any of these three outfits.

Blue Boat Company's boats depart from two locations: opposite the Heineken Experience at Stadhouderskade 550 and opposite the Hard Rock Café at Stadhouderskade 501 (€20, cheaper online; daily, every half-hour 10:00-18:00, fewer off-season; 1.25 hours, +31 20 679 1370, www.blueboat.nl).

Lovers boat lines offers basic one-hour canal cruises with narration, as well as dinner cruises. Boats depart right in front of Centraal station (€15; daily, every half-hour 10:00-21:00, fewer off-season; Prins Hendrikkade 25, +31 20 530 1090, www.lovers.nl).

Stromma offers similar one-hour cruises with three departure points: Centraal station, Rijksmuseum, and Damrak. All boats run from about 11:00-17:30 and all tickets are cheaper online (Centraal station—€17.50, runs April-Dec; Damrak Pier 5—€19.50, runs April-Dec; Rijksmuseum—€18.50, runs year-round; +31 20 217 0500, www.stromma.nl).

Smaller, Quirkier Canal Boat Tours

They are youthful, come with hip narration, encourage drinking, and are simply lots of fun.

Those Dam Boat Guys gives 1.5-hour tours with entertaining and knowledgeable guides (generally ex-pats who ask for tips). They encourage participants to bring a picnic (or drinks, or joints) and make a party of it (€29.50, not meant for younger kids, meet at their office at Prinsengracht 13, +31 202 101 669, reserve times at www.thosedamboatguys.com).

Friendship Amsterdam Boat Tours offers more standard one-hour tours in open boats that seat about 40 (€19, generally 3/hour—check website for times, Oudezijds Voorburgwal 230 in Red Light District, +31 20 334 4774, www.friendshipamsterdam.com).

Food Tours

Amsterdam has many competing food tours. A typical food tour will make six or eight stops in 3-4 hours and costs €80-100. They hit all the edible clichés (like pancakes, cheese, herring, Indonesian, apple pie, and Dutch gin) and come with fun commentary and the chance to meet local merchants. I enjoyed **Amsterdam Food Tours** (€87.50, 8 people max, +31 615 428 120, www.amsterdamfoodtours.com). You can comparison shop online: Check out **Hungry Birds** (www.hungrybirds.nl) or **Secret Food Tours** (www.secretfoodtours.com), or customize a tour with **Dennis Gerrits** (see "Private Guides," later).

Free City Walk

New Europe Tours "employs" native English-speaking students to give irreverent and entertaining two-hour walks. This long walk covers a lot of the city with an enthusiasm for the contemporary pot-and-prostitution scene, but walking tours are not allowed in the Red Light District (€1.50 charge for city's entertainment tax, tips expected, check schedule at www.neweuropetours.eu). All tours leave from the National Monument on Dam Square.

Private Guides

Mark Law, a knowledgeable guide who has clearly found his niche, offers three-hour small-group city walks for €35/person (up to 8 people). He also offers private tours (+31 627 269 604, www.thatdamguide.com, mark@thatdamguide.com).

    Dennis Gerrits is like a personal host who wants you to get the most out of your visit. His customized tours of Amsterdam and its surrounding cities and countryside can be by foot, bike, private boat, or car (from €50/hour, +31 6 3840 2919, www.lovemycitytours.com).

Private guides nourish your knowledge.

Guided bike tours cover lots of ground.

Do-It-Yourself Bike Tour of Amsterdam

For a good day trip, rent a bike at or near Centraal station. Head west down Haarlemmerstraat, working your wide-eyed way down Prinsengracht and detouring through the small, gentrified streets of the Jordaan neighborhood before popping out at the Westerkerk under the tallest spire in the city.

Pedal south to the lush and peaceful Vondelpark, then cut back through the center of town (Leidseplein to the Mint Tower, along Rokin street to Dam Square). From there, cruise the Red Light District, following Oudezijds Voorburgwal past the Old Church (Oude Kerk) to Zeedijk street, and return to the train station.

Then, you can escape into the countryside by hopping on the free ferry behind Centraal station. In five minutes, Amsterdam is gone, and you're rolling through your very own Dutch painting.

Albert Walet enjoys personalizing tours for Americans interested in getting to know his city. Al specializes in history, architecture, and water management, and exudes a passion for Amsterdam (€70/2 hours, €120/4 hours, up to 4 people, on foot or by bike, +31 6 2069 7882, abwalet2@yahoo.nl).

Larae Malooly will tailor a private tour to your interests, weaving in themes such as Renaissance architecture, Jewish heritage, and even local food (€185/up to 4 people for 4-hour Amsterdam tour, book at www.amsterdamsel.com).

Toms Travel Tours offers custom-designed private tours (€290/3 hours, +31 626 534 331, www.tomstraveltours.com, bookings@tomstraveltours.com).

Guided Bike Tours

Yellow Bike Guided Tours offers city bike tours of either two hours (€26, daily at 11:00, in winter at 13:30) or three hours (€31, daily at

ACTIVITIES

13:30), which both include a 20-minute break. All tours leave from Nieuwezijds Kolk 29, three blocks from Centraal station (reservations smart, +31 20 620 6940, www.yellowbike.nl).

SHOPPING

Amsterdam brings out the browser even in those who were not born to shop. The city has lots of one-of-a-kind specialty stores, street markets, and streets and neighborhoods worthy of a browse.

Souvenir Ideas: You won't need a guidebook to find plenty of shops selling wooden shoes, blue-and-white Delftware (ranging from inexpensive fireplace tiles to very expensive antiques), *jenever* (Dutch gin made from juniper berries, sold in traditional stone bottles), chocolate (Verkade or Droste cocoa in tins), or flower seeds and bulbs (be sure they're US Customs-friendly).

Department Stores

Hema is handy for everything from inexpensive clothes and notebooks to cosmetics. Stores are in the Kalvertoren shopping mall at Kalverstraat 212 and at Centraal station.

The **De Bijenkorf** department store, towering high above Dam Square, is Amsterdam's top-end option. The entire fifth floor is a ritzy self-service cafeteria with a rooftop terrace.

Open-Air Markets

Amsterdam's biggest open-air market, **Albert Cuyp,** stretching for several blocks along Albert Cuypstraat, bustles from roughly 9:00-17:00 every day except Sunday. You'll find fish, exotic vegetables, bolts of fabric, bargain clothes, native Dutch and international food stands. It's a 10-minute walk east of Museumplein and a block south of the Heineken Experience (tram #24).

While flower shops are scattered around the city, the most enjoyable browsing is at the **Flower Market,** which stretches luxuriously along the Singel canal between the Mint Tower and Koningsplein. The **Waterlooplein flea market** has stalls of garage-sale junk/treasure (Mon-Sat, near Waterlooplein Metro station).

Pretty petals at the floating Flower Market

Enjoy classical music at various venues.

Top Shopping Zones

The city's top shopping areas all have a different flavor.

The **Nine Little Streets** (De Negen Straatjes) are touristy, tidy, and central—hemmed in by a grid plan between Dam Square and the Jordaan. The area is home to a diverse array of shops mixing festive, inventive, nostalgic, practical, and artistic items. While ubiquitous chain stores are sneaking in (and it's not quite as artsy or funky as it once was), this zone remains a very convenient place to browse. For a preview, see www.de9straatjes.nl.

Haarlemmerstraat/Haarlemmerdijk, the area just west of Centraal station, has morphed from a bit grotty into a thriving and trendy string of shops, cafés, and restaurants. A browse here is a fun chance to spot new trends, and maybe to pick up some local clothes and goods (vintage and casual young fashions abound).

The lively street called **Staalstraat,** just east of the university zone, boasts an array of creative design shops, whimsical doodads, and vintage shops. The **Jordaan** is a mellow residential zone with a smattering of fine shops; on Mondays and Saturdays, it hosts the busy Noordermarkt market.

VAT and Customs

Getting a VAT Refund: If you purchase more than €50 worth of goods at a single store, you may be eligible to get a refund of the 21 percent Value-Added Tax (VAT). Get more details from your merchant or see RickSteves.com/vat.

Customs for American Shoppers: You can take home $800 worth of items per person duty-free, once every 31 days. You can bring in one liter of alcohol duty-free. For details on allowable goods, customs rules, and duty rates, visit Help.cbp.gov.

NIGHTLIFE

On summer evenings, people flock to the main squares for drinks at outdoor tables. Leidseplein is the liveliest square, surrounded by theaters, restaurants, and nightclubs. The slightly quieter Rembrandtplein (with adjoining Thorbeckeplein and nearby Reguliersdwarsstraat) is the center of gay clubs and nightlife. Spui features a full city block of bars. The Red Light District (particularly Oudezijds Achterburgwal) is less sleazy, even festive, in the early evening (before 22:30).

The TI's website, www.iamsterdam.com, has good English listings for upcoming events. Newsstands sell the *I Amsterdam* entertainment guide. The free calendar of events, *Uitkrant* (in Dutch), is available at TIs, bars, and bookstores.

Music
Classical Music: At lunchtime you'll find free classical music at the **Concertgebouw** at the far south end of Museumplein (+31 900 671 8345, www.concertgebouw.nl). For chamber music and contemporary works, visit the **Muziekgebouw aan 't IJ,** a mod concert hall on the waterfront, near the train station (Piet Heinkade 1, +31 20 788 2000, www.muziekgebouw.nl). For opera and dance, try the **opera house** in the Stopera building (Amstel 3, +31 20 625 5455, www.operaballet.nl). In the summer, Vondelpark hosts open-air concerts.

Also in summer, the **Westerkerk** has free lunchtime concerts most Wednesdays at 13:00, plus an annual Bach organ concert cycle in August (Prinsengracht 281, +31 20 624 7766, www.westerkerk.nl). The New Church offers periodic organ concerts and a religious music festival in June (Dam Square, +31 20 626 8168, www.nieuwekerk.nl). The Red Light District's Old Church (Oude Kerk) hosts occasional concerts, listed on their website (Oudekerksplein 23, +31 20 625 8284, www.oudekerk.nl).

Jazz: Jazz has a long tradition at the **Bimhuis** nightclub, housed in a black box jutting out from the Muziekgebouw performance hall, right on the waterfront. Its great bar has citywide views and is open to the public after concerts (Piet Heinkade 3, +31 20 788 2188, www.bimhuis.com).

Rock and Hip-Hop: The beat goes on at these two clubs, just off Leidseplein: **Paradiso** (Weteringschans 6, +31 20 626 4521, www.

paradiso.nl) and **Melkweg** (Lijnbaansgracht 234a, +31 20 531 8181, www.melkweg.nl). Both present big-name acts that you might recognize...if you're younger than me.

Comedy and Theater

Boom Chicago: This R-rated comedy improv act (in English) has been entertaining tourists and locals for years with rude, clever, and high-energy sketches mixed with improv games. If you need a break from museums and canal boat tours, this might be the ticket (€22-29, no shows Mon, in the Jordaan a couple of long blocks past Westerkerk at Rozengracht 117, +31 20 217 0400, www.boomchicago.nl).

   Theater: Amsterdam is one of the world centers for experimental live theater (much of it in English). Many theaters cluster around the street called the Nes, which stretches south from Dam Square. You can browse the offerings on the theaters' websites: **Vlaams Cultuurhuis de Brakke Grond** (www.brakkegrond.nl), **Frascati** (www.frascatitheater.nl), and **Tobacco Theater** (www.tobacco.nl).

Other Late-Night Fun

Movies: In the Netherlands most movies are subtitled, so English-only speakers have plenty of cinematic options. It's not unusual for movies at many cinemas to be sold out—consider buying tickets in advance. Catch a movie at the classic 1920s **Tuschinski Theater** (see page 127) or the splashy **EYE Filmmuseum Netherlands** (see page 134).

   Museums Open Late: The **Anne Frank House** is open daily until 22:00 (requires timed-entry ticket purchased in advance). Amsterdam's **marijuana** and **sex museums** stay open until at least 22:00.

   Skating After Dark: Amsterdammers get their skating fix every Friday night in Vondelpark. Huge groups don inline skates and meet at the round bench near the Vondel Pavilion (around 20:15, www.fridaynightskate.com). Anyone can join in. Ask your hotelier about the nearest place to rent skates, or try SkateDokter (www.skatedokter.nl).

Tuschinski Theater, a 1920s movie palace

Pot's on the menu at coffeeshops.

MARIJUANA (CANNABIS)

For tourists from lands where you can do hard time for lighting up, the open use of marijuana here can feel either somewhat disturbing, or exhilaratingly liberating...or maybe just normal. Several decades after being decriminalized in the Netherlands, marijuana causes about as much excitement here as a bottle of beer.

Marijuana Laws and "Coffeeshops"

Throughout the Netherlands, you'll see "coffeeshops"—cafés selling marijuana, with display cases showing various joints or baggies for sale. The retail sale of marijuana is strictly regulated, and proceeds are taxed. The minimum age for purchase is 18, and coffeeshops can sell up to five grams of marijuana per person per day. It's also illegal for these shops (or anyone) to advertise marijuana. In fact, in many places, the prospective customer must take the initiative and ask to see the menu of products for sale.

Shops sell marijuana and hashish both in pre-rolled joints and in little baggies. Joints are generally sold individually (€4-5, depending on whether it's hash with tobacco, marijuana with tobacco, or pure marijuana), though some places sell only small packs of three or four joints. Baggies generally contain a gram and go for €8-15.

Smoking Tips

Shops have loaner bongs and inhalers, and dispense rolling papers like toothpicks. While it's good style to ask first, if you're a paying customer (e.g., you buy a cup of coffee), you can generally pop into any coffeeshop and light up a joint, even if you didn't buy your pot there.

Don't ever buy pot on the street in Amsterdam. Well-established coffeeshops are considered much safer, and coffeeshop owners have an interest in keeping their trade safe and healthy.

The Dutch sell several forms of cannabis: They smoke both hashish (an extract of the cannabis plant) and the leaf of the plant (which they call "marihuana" or "grass"). While hash is mostly imported from Morocco, most of the marijuana sold in Dutch coffeeshops is grown locally, as coffeeshops find it's safer to deal with Dutch-grown plants than to import marijuana (the EU prohibits any international drug trade).

"Coffeeshops" in Amsterdam

Most of downtown Amsterdam's coffeeshops feel grungy and foreboding to American travelers who aren't part of the youth-hostel crowd. I've listed a few places with a more pub-like ambience for Americans wanting to go local, but within reason. Most purchases are in cash.

Paradox is the most *gezellig* (cozy), a mellow, graceful place whose staff are patient with descriptions and happy to walk you through all your options (two blocks from Anne Frank House at Eerste Bloemdwarsstraat 2, +31 20 623 5639, http://paradoxcoffeeshop.com). The flagship branch of the touristy **Bulldog Café coffeeshop** chain is in a former police station right on Leidseplein, offering alcohol upstairs and pot downstairs (Leidseplein 17, +31 20 625 6278, www.thebulldog.com). **Strain Hunters Coffeeshop,** conveniently located near Spui Square on Singel canal, has an inviting and friendly vibe (Singel 387, +31 20 624 7624).

Sleeping

I've grouped my hotel listings into several neighborhoods: **West Amsterdam** (quiet canals, charming gabled buildings), **Central Amsterdam** (shopping and tourist sights, though a bit gritty), and **Southwest Amsterdam** (a semi-suburban neighborhood around Vondelpark and Museumplein).

I like hotels that are clean, central, reasonably priced, friendly, small enough to have a hands-on owner and stable staff, and run with a respect for Dutch traditions.

Book as far in advance as possible. Amsterdam is jammed during tulip season (late March-mid-May), conventions, festivals, summer weekends, and some national holidays.

Amsterdam Hotels

Amsterdam is a tough city for budget accommodations, and any hotel room under €200 (or B&B room under €150) will have rough edges. Still, you can sleep well and safely in a great location for around €140 per double. Canalside rooms can come with great views—and early-morning construction-crew noise. Light sleepers should ask for a quiet room in the back.

Canal houses were built tight. They have steep stairs with narrow treads, and only some have elevators. If that's a problem, look for a hotel with an elevator—and confirm that it reaches your room. Hotels that don't have air-conditioning almost always have good fans.

Making Reservations

Reserve your rooms as soon as you've pinned down your travel dates. Book your room directly via email or phone, or through the hotel's official website. The hotelier wants to know:

- Type(s) of room(s) you want and number of guests
- Number of nights you'll stay
- Arrival and departure dates, written European-style as day/month/year (18/06/25 or 18 June 2025)
- Special requests (en suite bathroom, cheapest room, twin beds vs. double bed, quiet room)
- Applicable discounts (such as a Rick Steves discount, cash discount, or promotional rate)

Most places will request a credit-card number to hold your room. If the hotel's website doesn't have a secure form where you can enter the number directly, it's best to share this info via a phone call. If you must cancel, it's courteous—and smart—to do so with as much notice as possible. Cancellation policies can be strict; read the fine print. Always call or email to reconfirm your reservation a few days in advance. For B&Bs or very small hotels, I call again on my arrival day to tell my host what time I expect to get there (especially if arriving after 17:00).

Budget Tips

Comparison-shop by checking prices at several hotels (on each hotel's own website, on a booking site, or by email). For the best deal, book directly with the hotel. Ask for a discount if paying in cash; if the listing

Sleep Code

Dollar signs reflect average rates for a standard double room with breakfast in high season.

$$$$	**Splurge:** Most rooms over €260
$$$	**Pricier:** €200-260
$$	**Moderate:** €140-200
$	**Budget:** €70-140
¢	**Backpacker:** Under €70
RS%	**Rick Steves discount**

Unless otherwise noted, credit cards are accepted, hotel staff speak basic English, and free Wi-Fi is available. If the listing includes **RS%,** request a Rick Steves discount.

includes **RS%,** request a Rick Steves discount. Some hotels extend a discount to those who stay longer than three nights.

If you're staying in one place several nights, it's worth considering an apartment or rental house. These can be especially cost-effective for groups and families. European apartments, like hotel rooms, tend to be small by US standards. But they often come with laundry facilities and small, equipped kitchens, making it easier and cheaper to dine in. The city of Amsterdam limits the number of nights a property owner can rent out an entire apartment or house, making those harder to come by here than in other destinations. Websites such as Airbnb, FlipKey, Booking.com, and VRBO let you browse a wide range of properties.

For some travelers, traditional B&Bs or short-term, Airbnb-type rentals can be a good alternative; search for places in my recommended hotel neighborhoods. Some Amsterdam residents see vacation rentals as damaging to the fabric of traditionally residential neighborhoods. I like to counterbalance this trend by treating my temporary Amsterdam home—and neighbors—with a little extra courtesy.

WEST AMSTERDAM

Tree-lined canals, gabled buildings, and candlelit restaurants; just minutes on foot to Dam Square. Many of my hotels are old mansions—charming but with lots of steep stairs.

$$$$ The Toren Chandeliered mansion, pleasant canalside setting, peaceful backyard garden, classy yet friendly, on a quiet street, RS%—use code "RSSTEVES," breakfast extra, air-con, elevator.

Keizersgracht 164, +31 20 622 6033, www.thetoren.nl

$$$$ Hotel Ambassade Elegant, traditional yet modern, staff is top-notch, RS%, breakfast extra, air-con, elevator, some stairs.

Herengracht 341, +31 20 555 0222, www.ambassade-hotel.nl

$$$$ Hotel The Craftsmen Splurge hotel, beautifully decorated, reclaimed industrial decor, family rooms, air-con in most rooms, elevator.

Singel 83—entrance on Lijnbaanssteeg, +31 20 210 1218, http://hotelthecraftsmen.com

$$$$ 't Hotel Cozy 17th-century house, fresh rooms, garden and canal views, tearoom, family room, air-con.

Leliegracht 18, +31 20 422 2741, www.thotel.nl

$$$$ Mr. Jordaan Hotel In Greenwich Village-like neighborhood, funky-but-stylish rooms, some very snug, RS%—use code "enjoyjordaan" when booking, breakfast extra, air-con, elevator.

Bloemgracht 102, +31 20 626 5801, www.mrjordaan.nl

$$$ Linden Hotel Mr. Jordaan's sister hotel, tight teal-and-brown rooms, slightly cheaper, some canal views, RS%—use code "enjoylinden" when booking, breakfast extra, family rooms, air-con.

Lindengracht 251, +31 20 622 1460, www.lindenhotel.nl

$$$ Hotel Hegra Cozy, 17th-century merchant's house overlooking the canal, clean, modern, some rooms are small, some have canal views, no breakfast, family room.

Herengracht 269, +31 20 623 7877, www.hotelhegra.be

$$$ Hotel Hoksbergen Lower-priced option for a canalside setting, cramped rooms, bathrooms up to snuff, avoid very tight Room 4, family rooms.

Singel 301, +31 20 626 6043, www.hotelhoksbergen.com

$$ The Times Hotel Business-comfort hotel, canal setting, tight modern rooms, some have bathtubs, spare yet elegant, breakfast extra, family room, air-con, elevator.

Herengracht 135, +31 20 330 6030, www.thetimeshotel.com

$$ Max Brown Hotel Trendy urban design geared toward hipsters, quiet neighborhood near Centraal station, modern rooms and public areas, funky-chic details, spread over three canalside buildings.

Herengracht 13, +31 20 522 2345, www.maxbrownhotels.com

$$ Wiechmann Hotel Worn and sparsely furnished rooms, cozy public areas with Old World charm, lots of stairs, no elevator, some canal views, back rooms quiet.

Prinsengracht 328, +31 20 626 3321, www.hotelwiechmann.nl

$$ Herengracht 21 B&B Two stylish, intimate rooms in a canal house filled with art, traditional B&B run with care, private tours offered in 1920s-era canal boat.

Herengracht 21, +31 20 625 6305, www.herengracht21.nl

CENTRAL AMSTERDAM

Ideal for shopping, tourist sights, and public transportation, but the area has traffic noise and urban grittiness, and the hotels can lack character.

$$$ Hotel Ibis Amsterdam Centre Next to Centraal station, modern and efficient, comfort and value without a hint of charm, breakfast extra, book in advance, air-con, elevators.

Stationsplein 49, +31 20 721 9172, www.ibishotel.com

$$$ Hotel Résidence Le Coin Larger-than-average rooms with small kitchenettes, rooms slightly dated, breakfast extra, elevator.

Nieuwe Doelenstraat 5, +31 20 524 6800, www.lecoin.nl

$$ Hotel Nes Well-located, functional but bland, rooms are tight but modern, some canal views, breakfast extra, family room, elevator.

Kloveniersburgwal 137, +31 20 624 4773, www.hotelnes.com

SOUTHWEST AMSTERDAM

Semi-suburban neighborhood within walking distance of Vondelpark and Museumplein. Good-value modern accommodations (elevators) but less Old World charm.

$$$ Hotel Fita Bright and spacious rooms, close to Van Gogh Museum, modern yet rustic, espresso machines in every room, free breakfast when you book direct, air-con on some floors, elevator, free laundry service.

Jan Luijkenstraat 37, +31 20 679 0976, www.fita.nl

$$$ Bed & Breakfast Amsterdam Suite that sleeps up to four, clean and bright, full kitchen, balcony, canal views; cash, bank transfer, or PayPal only; not many stairs.

Sloterkade 65, +31 20 679 2753, www.bedandbreakfastamsterdam.net

$$ Hotel Alexander Modern hotel on a quiet street, garden patio, smart and clean, relaxed, breakfast extra, elevator, some stairs.

Vondelstraat 44, +31 20 589 4020, www.hotelalexander.nl

$$ Wildervanck B&B Two tastefully decorated rooms in elegant 17th-century canal house, run by friendly Dutch family, 2-night minimum, cash or bank transfer only, breakfast in pleasant dining room.

Keizersgracht 498, +31 20 623 3846, www.wildervanck.com

¢ Stayokay Vondelpark (IYHF) One of Amsterdam's top hostels, comfortable for all ages, some doubles, family rooms, lots of school groups, bike rental, right on Vondelpark.

Zandpad 5, +31 20 589 8996, www.stayokay.com

Eating

Amsterdam's thousand-plus eateries make for a buffet of dining options. Choose from elegant candlelit restaurants, an exotic Indonesian rijsttafel, a light meal outdoors alongside a canal, herring at a fish stand, or takeout "Flemish" fries with mayonnaise. Besides meals, the Dutch spend endless hours sitting and drinking at outdoor cafés. Budget some money—and time—to sightseeing for your palate.

My listings are in Amsterdam's atmospheric neighborhoods, handy to recommended hotels and sights. Most are in **Central Amsterdam** (around Dam Square, Spui, and the Mint Tower), **West Amsterdam** (near the Anne Frank House and the Jordaan—the most charming place to dine), and **Southwest Amsterdam** (close to the museum quarter).

No matter where you dine, expect it to be *gezellig*—a much-prized Dutch virtue, meaning an atmosphere of relaxed coziness.

Restaurant Code

Dollar signs reflect the cost of a typical main course.

$$$$ **Splurge:** Most main courses over €30
$$$ **Pricier:** €20-30
$$ **Moderate:** €10-20
$ **Budget:** Under €10

A *friets* stand or other takeout spot is **$**; a basic café or sit-down eatery is **$$**; a casual but more upscale restaurant is **$$$**; and a swanky splurge is **$$$$**.

When in Amsterdam...

I eat on the Dutch schedule. For breakfast, I eat at the hotel (bread, meat, cheese, eggs) or grab a pastry and coffee at a café. Lunch (12:00-14:00) is a simple sandwich (*broodje*) or soup. In between meals, I might stop at a takeout stand for French fries (*friets*) or a pickled herring. In the late afternoon, Amsterdammers enjoy a beverage with friends at an outdoor table on a lively square. Dinner (18:00-21:00) is the biggest meal of the day, the time for slowing down and savoring a multicourse restaurant meal.

In this extremely touristy city with its cruise groups, English stag parties, and masses of low-end travelers, it's important to avoid sloppy tourist ghettos. With a bike or a willingness to walk 10 minutes, you can easily leave the tourist zone and find more rewarding dining experiences. If you eat in the Leidseplein area or along Damrak, it's your own fault.

Restaurants

As English is spoken everywhere, and the Dutch take an elegant-but-casual approach to dining, there's no need to learn a lot of special Dutch etiquette. At Dutch restaurants that have waitstaff, 15 percent service is included in the menu price, although it's common to round up the bill after a good meal (usually 5-10 percent). The Dutch are willing to pay for bottled water with their meal (Spa brand is popular, sparkling or still), but free tap water is always available upon request.

Cafés and Bars

Besides full-service restaurants, there are other places to fill the tank.

A café, or eetcafé, is a simple restaurant serving basic soups, salads, and sandwiches, as well as traditional meat-and-potatoes meals in a generally comfortable but no-nonsense setting. A *salon de thé* serves tea and coffee, but also pastries and sandwiches. At night, cafés are essentially "bars," catering to the drinking crowd.

Bruin cafés ("brown cafés") are named for their nicotine-stained walls—until smoking was banned indoors in 2008, they were filled with tobacco smoke. They are usually more bar-like, with dimmer lighting and wood paneling. A *proeflokaal* is a bar (with snacks) offering wine, spirits, or beer. A "coffeeshop" is a café where marijuana is sold and consumed, though most offer drinks and munchies, too.

Cafés and bars with outdoor tables generally charge the same whether you sit inside or out. When ordering drinks in a café or bar, you can just pay as you go (especially if the bar is crowded), or wait until the end to settle up, as many locals do. If you get table service, take the cue from your server. There's no need to tip if you order at the

Most cafés and bars won't charge you more for dining outdoors.

Edam and Gouda—common Dutch cheeses

Herring sandwich—what's not to love?

counter, but if you get table service, it's nice to round up to the next euro ("keep the change").

Most cafés have a light-fare menu of sandwiches, salads, and soups, but some offer more ambitious meals. Throughout the day they cater to customers who just want to relax over a drink.

The Dutch love their coffee, enjoying many of the same drinks (espresso, cappuccino) served in American or Italian coffee shops. A *koffie verkeerd* (fer-KEERT, "coffee wrong") is an espresso with a lot of steamed milk. Many cafés/bars have a juicer for making fresh-squeezed orange juice, and they'll have the full array of soft drinks.

Order "a beer," and you'll get a *pils*—a light pilsner-type beer in a 10-ounce glass with a thick head leveled off with a stick. Typical brands are Heineken, Grolsch, Oranjeboom, Amstel, and the mis-named Bavaria (brewed in Holland). Belgian beers are also popular.

The Dutch enjoy a chilled shot of *jenever* (yah-NAY-ver), a Dutch gin made from juniper berries. *Jong* (young) is sharper; *oude* (old) is mellow and more expensive. You'll find a variety of local fruit brandies and cognacs. The Dutch people drink a lot of fine wine, but it's almost all imported.

Picnicking

Amsterdam makes it easy to turn a picnic into a first-class affair. Grab something to go and enjoy a bench in a lively square or with canalside ambience.

Sandwiches (*broodjes*) of delicious cheese or ham on fresh bread are cheap at snack bars and delis. You'll find takeout stands selling herring, French fries, and international foods.

Albert Heijn grocery stores have great deli sections with picnic-perfect takeaway salads and sandwiches. There are handy locations near Museumplein, Dam Square, the Mint Tower, on the corner of Leidsestraat and Singel, and inside Centraal station.

Traditional Dutch Cuisine

Traditional Dutch cooking is basic and hearty—meat or fish, soup, fresh bread, boiled potatoes, cooked vegetables, and salad. Mashed potato dishes (*stamppot* or *hutspot*) served with meat and vegetables is classic Dutch comfort food. But these days, many Dutch people have traveled and become more sophisticated, enjoying dishes from around the world.

The Dutch are better known for their informal foods. Pickled herring (*haring*) comes with onions or pickles on a bun. French fries (*Vlaamse friets*) are eaten with mayonnaise rather than ketchup. Popular Dutch cheeses are Edam (covered with red wax) or Gouda (HOW-dah). *Kroketten* (croquettes) are log-shaped rolls of meats and vegetables (kind of like corn dogs) breaded and deep-fried. *Pannenkoeken* (pancakes) can be either sweet dessert pancakes or crêpe-like, savory pancakes eaten as a meal.

For dessert, try *pannenkoeken, poffertjes* (small, sugared puffy

Eat, drink, and be merry on city squares.

International treat—Middle Eastern shish kebab   *Pannenkoeken* can be sweet or savory.

pancakes), *stroopwafels* (syrup waffles), and *appelgebak* or *appeltaart* (apple pie).

International

Since its golden age days as a global trader, Amsterdam has adopted food from other lands.

Indonesian *(Indisch)*, from this former Dutch colony, is commonly served as a rijsttafel (literally, "rice table"), a multidish sampler of many spicy dishes and rice or noodles. A *rijsttafel* is huge—generally more food than you can comfortably eat. Many restaurants require a two-person minimum order. Other Indonesian menu items *(nasi rames, bami goreng, nasi goreng)* are also multidish meals. Common Indonesian sauces are peanut, red chili *(sambal)*, and dark soy.

You'll also find Middle Eastern *shoarma* (roasted lamb in pita bread), falafel, gyros, or a *döner kebab*.

Surinamese *(Surinaamse)*, from the former colony on the northeast coast of South America, is a mix of Caribbean and Indonesian influences. The signature dish is *roti* (spiced chicken wrapped in flatbread) and rice (white or fried) served with meats in sauces (curry and spices).

Alstublieft: Wherever you eat in Amsterdam—at fine restaurants, dim cafés, or the pickled herring shack—you'll constantly hear servers saying *"Alstublieft"* (AHL-stoo-bleeft). It's a useful, catch-all polite word, meaning "please," "here's your order," "enjoy," and "you're welcome." You can respond by saying, *"Dank u wel"* (dahnk oo vehl)—thank you.

CENTRAL AMSTERDAM

Eateries along the spine of the old center, from Spui, Rokin, and the Mint Tower to Dam Square and Centraal station (see the map in this chapter).

1 **$$$$ Restaurant Hemelse Modder** Fine-dining splurge, beautifully situated on canal, subdued vibe, multicourse tasting menus only, reservations required, closed Sun.

Oude Waal 11, +31 20 624 3203, www.hemelsemodder.nl

2 **$$$ The Seafood Bar** Fresh and fishy, popular—reserve ahead, mixed platters for sharing, several locations around town, daily.

Spui 15, +31 20 233 7452, www.theseafoodbar.nl

3 **$$$$ Restaurant d'Vijff Vlieghen** Dressy museum of a restaurant, romantic splurge, Dutch and international cuisine, closed Mon-Tue.

Spuistraat 294, +31 20 530 4060

4 **$ Singel 404 Lunch Café** Sweet little café; burgers, bagel sandwiches, and more; daily until 18:00.

Singel 404, +31 20 428 0154

5 **$$$ Café Luxembourg** Old bistro, "grand café" interior, basic fare, famous for croquettes and burgers, long hours daily.

Spui 24, +31 20 620 6264

6 **$$ Van Kerkwijk** Quirky eatery, no written menu—server explains offerings, freshly prepared international dishes, daily.

Nes 41, +31 20 620 3316

7 **$$ Gartine** Hidden gem, brunch until noon, classy spot for a light meal or high tea; Wed-Sun until 17:00, closed Mon-Tue.

Taksteeg 7, +31 20 320 4132

8 **$$ Pannenkoekenhuis Upstairs** Tight, tiny, characteristic perch up steep stairs, delicious pancakes, daily until 18:00.

Grimburgwal 2, +31 20 626 5603

9 **$$ Café 't Gasthuys** Brown café, canalside seating, busy dumbwaiter cranks out light lunches, sandwiches, and basic dinners, daily.

Grimburgwal 7, +31 20 624 8230

10 **$$$ De Jaren Café** Big, modern local favorite; soups, salads, and sandwiches; canalside patio, long hours daily.

Nieuwe Doelenstraat 20, +31 20 625 5771

11 **$$ Blue Amsterdam Restaurant** Shopping-mall diner, good views; soups, salads, and vegetarian dishes; daily until 18:30.

In Kalverpassage shopping mall, +31 20 427 3901

EATING

WEST AMSTERDAM

Charming canals near the Anne Frank House and Jordaan residential neighborhood (see the map in this chapter).

⑫ **$$$ Café Restaurant de Reiger** Famous for fresh fish, ribs, and good beer on tap; bistro ambience, closed Sun-Mon.
Nieuwe Leliestraat 34, +31 20 624 7426

⑬ **$$$ Amoi** Upscale, modern bar; traditional and delicious Indonesian fare, full rijsttafel not offered, good à la carte menu, reservations smart, closed Mon-Tue.
Kinkerstraat 53a, +31 20 846 2755, https://amoiamsterdam.nl

⑭ **$$$$ Max Restaurant** Upscale Indonesian food fused with French influences, fine rijsttafel tasting menu, reservations recommended, closed Sun-Tue.
Herenstraat 14, +31 20 420 0222, www.maxrestaurant.nl

⑮ **$$ Sonneveld Eetcafe,** Traditional fare, ribs and stamppot, good salads, sidewalk seating, daily.
Tweede Egelantiersdwarsstraat 72, +31 20 423 4287

⑯ **$$$ Ristorante Toscanini** Popular, upmarket Italian, lively and spacious, great cuisine, reservations essential, closed Mon.
Lindengracht 75, +31 20 623 2813, http://restauranttoscanini.nl

⑰ **$$$ Restaurant Moeders** Homey menu, tight interior, Dutch and international home cooking, reservations smart, Mon-Fri dinner only, Sat-Sun lunch and dinner.
Rozengracht 251, +31 20 626 7957, www.moeders.com

⑱ **$$ La Perla** Wood-fired pizza, few tables but another dining room across the street, sidewalk seating, daily.
Tweede Tuindwarsstraat 14 and 53, reserve online, www.pizzaperla.nl

⑲ **$ Café 't Smalle** Canalside brown café; simple meals of soups, salads, and sandwiches; daily, bar snacks only after 17:00.
Egelantiersgracht 12, +31 20 623 9617

⑳ **$$ Café de Prins** Brown café with outdoor seating on canal, poffertjes—tiny Dutch pancakes—and simple bar food, long hours daily.
Prinsengracht 124, +31 20 624 9382

㉑ **$$ Café Winkel** Sloppy and youthful, hearty plates, rustic interior, casual tables on open square, famous appeltaart, long hours daily.
Noordermarkt 43, +31 20 623 0223

㉒ **$$ Café van Zuylen** Perfect for people watching; salads, burgers, local standards, Dutch and Belgian beers on tap; long hours daily.
Torensteeg 4, +31 20 639 1055

SOUTHWEST AMSTERDAM

Near Museumplein, Vondelpark, and Leidseplein (see the map on page 124).

(see the map on page 124)

$$$$ Restaurant Blauw Upmarket Indonesian cuisine including rijsttafel, bright and modern, near Vondelpark, daily.

Amstelveenseweg 158, +31 20 675 50 00

$$ Renzo's Italian delicatessen, good sandwiches, prepared pasta dishes, pay extra to sit at tables, long hours daily.

Van Baerlestraat 67, +31 20 763 1673

$$ 'T Blauwe Theehuis Vondelpark teahouse, drinks and light meals, long hours daily.

Vondelpark 5, +31 20 662 0254

$$$ De Balie Grand Café Ground-floor eatery in a gallery and concert venue; salads, sandwiches, and simple plates; daily.

Kleine-Gartmanplantsoen 10, +31 20 553 5130

$$$ Buffet van Odette Elegant, Mediterranean and Italian cuisine, healthy, unpretentious, romantic and peaceful, closed Sun-Tue.

Prinsengracht 598, +31 20 423 6034

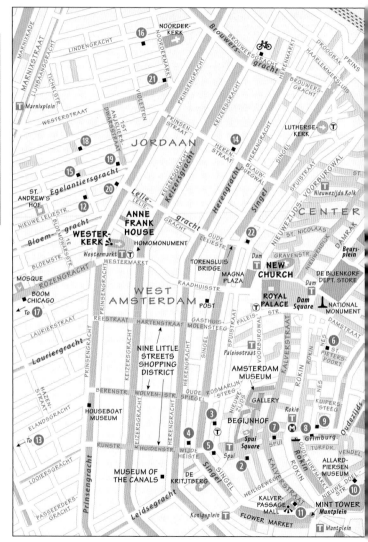

Amsterdam Restaurants

To NDSM Pier
To Buiksloterweg,
Eye Filmmuseum
& A-dam Tower
To IJPlein
Centraal Stn.
Centraal Stn.
Centraal Stn.
DE RUIJTERKADE
IBIS HOTEL
BIKE GARAGE
HENDRIKKADE
CENTRAAL STATION
Het IJ (Channel)
200 Meters
200 Yards
N
Stationsplein
Central Station Westzijde
Central Station Oostzijde
DE RUIJTERKADE
To Cruise Terminal
DAMRAK SEX MUSEUM
PRINS HENDRIKKADE
ST. NICOLAAS
WEEPERS' TOWER
SKY-LOUNGE AMST.
OOSTERDOKSTR.
DAMRAK
JACOBS
NIEUWEBRUG
ZEEDIJK
OUDEZIJDS KOLK
OUDEBRUG
OOSTERDOKSKADE
CENTRAL LIBRARY (OPENBARE BIBLIOTHEEK AMSTERDAM)
STOCK EXCHANGE (BEURS)
OUR LORD IN THE ATTIC MUSEUM
KROMME WAAL
Oosterdok
Damrak
LANGE NIEZEL
GELDERSKADE
OLD CHURCH
STORMSTEEG
EROTIC MUSEUM
PRINS HENDRIKKADE
NEMO (SCIENCE MUSEUM)
ST. ANNEN STR.
Voorburgwal
MOLEN-STEEG
WARMOESSTR.
BINNEN
KANT
KALKMARKT
RED LIGHT DISTRICT
WAAG
BLOED-STR.
Nieuwmarkt
Nieuw-markt
Waalseilandsgracht
OUDE WAAL
NORTHEAST AMSTERDAM
HASH MUSEUM
Oudezijds
BARNDE-STEEG
KOESTR.
BETH. STRAAT
HOOGSTR.
ST. ANTONIESBREESTR.
DIJKSTR.
OUDESCHANS
Oude schans
NIEUWE UILENBURGERSTR.
PEPER-STRAAT
RAPENBURG
FOELIESTRAAT
Achterburgwal
Kloveniersburgwal
RUSLAND
RAAMGRACHT
TAKST.
N.Z.
Uilenburgergracht
VALKENBURGER-STRAAT
NIEUWE UILENBURGERGRACHT
AMST. UNIVERSITY
REMBRANDT HOUSE
GASSAN DIAMONDS
SOUTHEAST AMSTERDAM
STAALSTR.
Waterloo-plein
MOSES & AARON CHURCH
Meester Visserplein
PORTUGUESE SYNAGOGUE
Meester Visserplein
DUTCH RESISTANCE MUSEUM
STAALKADE
OPERA HOUSE
Amstel
AMSTEL
Waterloo-plein
NIEUWE AMSTEL STR.
JEWISH HISTORY MUSEUM
Zwanenburgwal
MIDDENLAAN
DUTCH THEATER

Practicalities

Travel Tips

Travel Advisories: Before traveling, check updated health and safety conditions, including restrictions for your destination, at Travel.State. gov (US State Department's travel pages) and CDC.gov (Centers for Disease Control and Prevention).

Tourist Information: Amsterdam's TI, on Centraal station's IJ side (follow signs for *IJ-zijde*), is called the "I Amsterdam Store"—but it's an official TI. It's generally crowded and sometimes inefficient, but staff are helpful. You can buy a good city map (skip the free version) and the *I Amsterdam* entertainment guide here (Mon-Fri 10:00-19:00, Sat-Sun 9:00-18:00, +31 20 702 6000).

Language Barrier: This is one of the easiest places in the non-English-speaking world for an English speaker. Nearly all signs and services are offered in two languages: Dutch and "non-Dutch" (i.e., English).

Shop Hours: Most stores are open from about 9:00 until 17:00 (or 18:00) on weekdays. Some open at 12:00 on Mondays and Sundays. Shops may stay open until 21:00 on Thursdays.

Time Zones: The Netherlands is six/nine hours ahead of the East/West Coasts of the US. For a handy time converter, use the world clock app on your phone or download one (see www.timeanddate. com).

Watt's Up? Europe's electrical system is 220 volts, instead of North America's 110 volts. Most electronics (laptops, phones, cameras) and appliances (hair dryers, CPAP machines) convert automatically, so you won't need a converter, but you will need an adapter plug with two round prongs, sold inexpensively at travel stores in the US.

Safety and Emergencies

Emergency and Medical Help: For any emergency service—ambulance, police, or fire—call 112 from a mobile phone or landline. If you get sick, do as the Dutch do and go to a pharmacist for advice (see listings on the next page). Or ask at your hotel for help—they'll know the nearest medical and emergency services.

Theft or Loss: The city has more than its share of pickpockets—especially in the train station, on trams, in and near crowded

Helpful Websites

Netherlands Tourist Information: Holland.com
Amsterdam Tourist Information: IAmsterdam.com
Passports and Red Tape: Travel.State.gov
Flights: Flights.Google.com (international flights), SkyScanner.com (flights within Europe)
Airplane Carry-on Restrictions: TSA.gov
Train Schedules: Bahn.com
General Travel Tips: RickSteves.com (train travel, rail passes, car rental, travel insurance, packing lists, and more)

museums, at places of drunkenness, and at many hostels. Wear your money belt.

To replace a **passport,** you'll need to go in person to the US consulate (+31 70 310 2209, Museumplein 19, https://nl.usembassy.gov). If your credit and debit cards disappear, cancel and replace them, and report the loss immediately (with a mobile phone, call these 24-hour US numbers: Visa +1 303 967 1096, Mastercard +1 636 722 7111, and American Express +1 336 393 1111). For more information, see RickSteves.com/help.

Street Smarts: Beware of silent transportation—trams, electric mopeds, and bicycles—when walking around Amsterdam. Before you step off a sidewalk, double-check both directions to make sure all's clear.

Around Town

English Bookstores: For fiction and guidebooks, try the **American Book Center** at Spui 12, right on the square. The huge and helpful **Scheltema** is near Dam Square at Rokin 9. **Waterstone's Booksellers,** a UK chain, also sells British newspapers; it's near Spui at 152 Kalverstraat.

Maps: Given the city's maze of streets and canals, you'll want a good city map. I like the *Carto Studio Centrumkaart Amsterdam* map. You can download offline maps from **City Maps 2Go** and **Google Maps.**

Pharmacy: The shop named **DA** (Dienstdoende Apotheek) sells basic toiletries and has a pharmacy counter in the back (Leidsestraat

74 near where it meets Prinsengracht, +31 20 627 5351). Near Dam Square, there's **BENU Apotheek** (Damstraat 2, +31 20 624 4331).

Laundry: Try **Clean Brothers Wasserette** in the Jordaan (daily, Westerstraat 26, one block from Prinsengracht, +31 20 627 9888) or **Powders,** near Leidseplein (daily, Kerkstraat 56, one block south of Leidsestraat, +31 6 1080 1859).

ARRIVAL IN AMSTERDAM

Schiphol Airport

Schiphol Airport (SKIP-pol, code: AMS, www.schiphol.nl), about 10 miles southwest of Amsterdam's city center, is user-friendly. Though Schiphol officially has four terminals, it's really just one big building. You could walk it end to end in about 20 minutes (but allow plenty of time to pass through security checkpoints between terminals). Interactive info kiosks and the Schiphol app have handy maps to find nearby services and eateries. All terminals have free Wi-Fi.

Baggage-claim areas for all terminals empty into the same central zone, officially called Schiphol Plaza but generally signed *Arrivals Hall.* Here you'll find a busy TI (near Terminal 2, daily 7:00-22:00), and transportation options: train, bus, taxi, and Uber. Convenient luggage lockers are at various points (both short- and long-term lockers, cash and cards accepted; biggest bank of lockers near the train station at Schiphol Plaza).

If you'll be traveling by rail, take advantage of the **"Train Tickets and Services"** counter (Schiphol Plaza ground level, across from Burger King).

To get between Schiphol and downtown Amsterdam, you have several options:

By Train: Direct trains to Amsterdam's Centraal station run frequently from Schiphol Plaza (4-6/hour, 20 minutes, €5.70). Schiphol's train station also serves other destinations, including Delft, The Hauge, Rotterdam, Bruges, and Brussels. If you're only going to Amsterdam, consider the **Amsterdam Travel Ticket.** It covers city trams, buses, and the train ride to and from Schiphol (€17/1 day, multiday options, http://en.gvb.nl/amsterdam-travel-ticket). The I Amsterdam City Card, a sightseeing pass, also covers all tram, bus, and Metro travel

Schiphol Airport is a quick train ride...

...from Amsterdam's Centraal station.

within Amsterdam (see "Advance Tickets and Sightseeing Passes" on page 122).

By Public Bus: Connexxion #397 is handy for those going to the Leidseplein district (€6.50, buy ticket from driver—credit card only, departs from lane B17 in front of the airport).

By Taxi or Uber: Allow about €50 to downtown Amsterdam by regular **taxi. Uber** serves the airport for about €36.

Centraal Train Station

The portal connecting Amsterdam to the world is its aptly named Centraal station. From here you're within walking distance of Dam Square, and all the transportation options (tram, bus, taxi, Metro, and rental bikes) are right out front.

The station is fully equipped. Luggage lockers are in the east corridor, under the "B" end of the platforms (open 5:00-00:45, can fill up on busy summer weekends). You'll also find plenty of shops, eateries, and "to go" supermarkets. The Service Point store in the northern section is a handy place to buy phone accessories, mail a package, or print a ticket (daily 7:00-22:00). You can buy tickets for Amsterdam's public-transport system from machines labeled *Tram Bus Metro Tickets.* Exiting the station, you're in the heart of the city. Straight ahead is Damrak street, leading to Dam Square (a 10-minute walk). Taxis are behind the station on the northwest side.

By Tram, Bus, and Metro

Amsterdam's public-transit system (GVB) includes trams, buses, and an underground Metro. Of these, trams are most useful for most tourists. For transit information, visit the OV Service and Tickets office, a few doors to the left of the I Amsterdam store at Centraal station. Here you can use travel-planning kiosks, buy and print train tickets, and pick up maps (Mon-Fri 7:00-21:00, Sat-Sun 8:00-18:00, +31 307 515 155).

The GVB website has a journey planner and route map (www. gvb.nl). Google Maps or the Citymapper app both show your transit options (Citymapper comes with offline public-transit maps).

Tickets and Passes: A one-hour ticket costs €3.20 and is good on the tram, bus, and Metro, including transfers. A pass is more economical if you're staying in Amsterdam for a few days and riding a lot of trams. Passes good for unlimited city transit are available for 24 hours (€8.50), 48 hours (€14.50), 72 hours (€20), and 96 hours (€25.50). There are also passes that cover both the tram-bus-Metro system and train rides in the Netherlands (discussed below).

Buy tickets and day passes from machines at most tram stops, or on board all buses and most trams (credit card only, usually at the rear of the tram or bus; if there's no conductor, pay driver). The full range of tickets and passes is also available at Metro-station vending machines and TIs.

If you plan to make day trips outside Amsterdam, consider the Amsterdam & Region Travel Ticket. This covers in-city trams and buses, as well as trains to nearby destinations such as Haarlem, Zaanse Schans, Edam, Volendam, Marken (by bus), Aalsmeer, and Schiphol Airport. If you do two or more day trips, the 2- or 3-day passes can save you a little money and the hassle of buying individual tickets (€28/2 days, €36.50/3 days; one-day pass not worth it); sold at TIs and at ticket machines at Schiphol Airport and Centraal station (on the IJ-Hall/ north side; www.iamsterdam.com).

Trams: Trams are easy. You can buy tickets from machines inside Centraal station (coins or credit cards). Or simply hop on, buy your ticket on board (ticket booth is usually in the back, credit cards only), and you're on your way. Board the tram at any door not marked with a red/white "do not enter" sticker. Once aboard, you must immediately

Get a bike—it's how locals roll.

Trams connect you to many sights and hotels.

"check in" by touching your pass or ticket to one of the pink-and-gray scanners. (If you buy your ticket from the conductor at the back of the tram, you must still "check in" with your ticket once you have it.) The scanner will beep and flash a green light after a successful scan. Be careful not to accidentally scan your ticket or pass twice while boarding, or it becomes invalid. Just before exiting, you must "check out" by scanning it again.

Trams #2 and #12 travel north-south, connecting Centraal station, the Jordaan neighborhood, many of my recommended hotels, and Leidseplein. Both trams then continue beyond Leidseplein to Museumplein (the stop for the Rijksmuseum and Van Gogh Museum). Tram #14 runs south-east, connecting Centraal station to Rembrandtplein, Waterlooplein, and Alexanderplein, and Southeast Amsterdam sights. To get to the Anne Frank House and the Jordaan, take tram #13 or #17 from Centraal station (or Dam Square) to Westermarkt.

Buses and Metro: Tickets and passes work on buses and the Metro as they do on the trams—pay with a credit card and scan your ticket or pass as you enter and again when you leave. The Metro system is limited and used mostly for commuting to the suburbs—but it does loosely connect Centraal station with some sights to the south and east of Damrak.

By Bike

You'll get around town by bike faster than you can by taxi. Everyone—bank managers, students, pizza-delivery workers, and police—uses bikes to get around. It's by far the smartest way to travel in a city where 40 percent of all traffic rolls on two wheels. One-speed bikes, with *"brrringing"* bells and foot brakes, rent for about €10 per day (cheaper for longer periods) at any number of places—hotels can send you to the nearest spot.

Star Bikes Rental has cheap rates and long hours (De Ruijterkade 143, +31 20 620 3215, www.starbikesrental.com). **MacBike** has an efficient outlet at Centraal station as well as three smaller locations (free rental with I Amsterdam City Card, at east end of station—on the left as you exit; +31 20 624 8391, www.macbike.nl). Frédéric Rent-a-Bike, a 10-minute walk from Centraal station, has quality bikes and a helpful staff (RS%-10 percent discount, Binnen Wieringerstraat 23, +31 20 624 5509, www.frederic.nl).

Biking Tips: No one here wears a helmet. They do, however, ride cautiously, and so should you: Use arm signals, follow the bike-only traffic signals, stay in the obvious and omnipresent bike lanes, and yield to traffic on the right. Fear oncoming trams and tram tracks. Obey all traffic signals and walk your bike through pedestrian zones (fines are reportedly €80). Google Maps includes bicycles as a mode of transportation for the Netherlands. For bike tours, see "Guided Bike Tours" in the Activities chapter.

By Boat

Lovers boat lines shuttle tourists on **hop-on, hop-off** routes covering different combinations of the city's top sights. Most routes come with recorded narration (€27.50/24-hour pass, roughly every 20 minutes, 2 hours, +31 20 530 1090, www.lovers.nl).

By Taxi and Uber

Given the good tram system and ease of biking, I use taxis less in Amsterdam than any other city in Europe. The city's taxis have a drop charge (about €3), after which it's €2.19 per kilometer. You can wave them down, find a rare taxi stand, call one (+31 20 777 7777), or download their app (Taxi Amsterdam "TaxiTCA"). Uber works in Amsterdam like in the US.

By Car

If you have a car, park it—all you'll find are frustrating one-way streets, terrible parking, and meter readers with a passion for booting cars. Pay to park safely in a central garage. Better, leave the car at one of the city's supervised suburban park-and-ride lots (follow *P&R* signs from freeway).

Tipping

Tipping in the Netherlands isn't as automatic and generous as it is in the US, but some general guidelines apply.

Restaurants: Tipping is an issue only at restaurants that have table service. If paying with a credit card, be prepared to tip separately with cash or coins; credit-card receipts don't have a tip line.

Taxis: For a typical ride, round up your fare a bit (for instance, if the fare is €4.50, pay €5).

Services: For local guides, private drivers, or others who spend several hours with you, and significantly improve the quality of your trip, a healthy tip (of around 10 percent) is not extravagant. In general, if someone in the tourism or service industry does a super job for you, a small tip of a euro or two is appropriate. If you're not sure whether (or how much) to tip for a service, ask a local for advice.

MONEY

The Netherlands uses the euro currency: 1 euro (€) = about $1.10. To convert prices in euros to dollars, add about 10 percent: €20 = about $22, €50 = about $55. Check Oanda.com for the latest exchange rates.

You'll use your **credit card** for purchases both big (hotels, advance tickets) and small (little shops, food stands). A "tap-to-pay" or "contactless" card is widely accepted and simple to use. Check to see if you already have—or can get—a tap-to-pay version of your credit card (look on the card for the tap-to-pay symbol—four curvy lines). Make sure you know the numeric four-digit PIN for each of your cards, both debit and credit. Request it if you don't have one, as it may be required for some purchases.

Use a **debit card** at ATMs to withdraw a small amount of local cash. Be aware that many ATMs in heavily touristed areas are often operated by for-profit companies with unfavorable exchange rates—most notably Travelex and Euronet. Schiphol Airport's ATMs are primarily run by Travelex and have terrible exchange rates. You'll get better rates in town at yellow Geldmaat ATMs (use the "Locate" feature at www.geldmaat.nl to find the nearest one) or at a **bank** ATM; major Dutch banks include ABN AMRO, ING, and Rabobank. While many transactions are by card these days, cash can help you out of a jam if your card randomly doesn't work, and can be useful to pay for things like tips and local guides. Keep your cards and cash safe in a money belt.

At self-service payment machines (such as transit-ticket kiosks), US cards may not work. In this case, look for a cashier who can process your card manually—or pay in cash.

STAYING CONNECTED

Making International Calls
From a Mobile Phone: Phone numbers in this book are presented exactly as you would dial them from a US mobile phone. For international access, press and hold 0 (zero) to get a + sign, then dial the country code (31 for the Netherlands) and phone number.

From a US Landline to Europe: Replace + with 011 (US/Canada access code), then dial the country code (31 for the Netherlands) and phone number.

From a European Landline to the US or Europe: Replace + with 00 (Europe access code), then dial the country code (31 for the Netherlands, 1 for the US) and phone number. For more phoning help, see HowToCallAbroad.com.

Using Your Phone in Europe
Sign up for an international plan. To stay connected at a lower cost, sign up for an international service plan through your carrier. Most providers offer a simple bundle that includes calling, messaging, and data.

Use free Wi-Fi whenever possible. Unless you have an unlimited-data plan, save most of your online tasks for Wi-Fi. Most accommodations in Europe offer free Wi-Fi, and many cafés offer hotspots for customers. You may also find Wi-Fi at TIs, city squares, major museums, public-transit hubs, airports, and aboard trains and buses.

Save large-data tasks for Wi-Fi. If your included data is slow or metered, wait until you're on Wi-Fi to Skype or FaceTime, download apps, stream videos, or do other megabyte-greedy tasks. Using a navigation app such as Google Maps over a cellular network can require lots of data, so download maps when you're on Wi-Fi, then use the app offline.

Use Wi-Fi calling and messaging apps. Skype, FaceTime, and Google Meet are great for making free or low-cost calls or sending texts over Wi-Fi worldwide. WhatsApp is especially popular with Europeans, and is often the easiest way to communicate with guides, drivers, or other local contacts.

RESOURCES FROM RICK STEVES

Begin your trip at RickSteves.com. This book is just one of many in my series on European travel. I also produce a public television series, *Rick Steves' Europe,* and a public radio show, *Travel with Rick Steves.* My mobile-friendly website is *the* place to explore Europe in preparation for your trip. You'll find thousands of fun articles, beautiful photos, videos, and radio interviews; a wealth of money-saving tips; travel news dispatches; a video library of travel talks; our latest guidebook updates (RickSteves.com/update); and the free Rick Steves Audio Europe app with audio tours of Europe's top sights. You can also follow me on Facebook, Instagram, and Twitter.

Packing Checklist

Clothing

- ❑ 5 shirts: long- & short-sleeve
- ❑ 2 pairs pants (or skirts/capris)
- ❑ 1 pair shorts
- ❑ 5 pairs underwear & socks
- ❑ 1 pair walking shoes
- ❑ Sweater or warm layer
- ❑ Rainproof jacket with hood
- ❑ Tie, scarf, belt, and/or hat
- ❑ Swimsuit
- ❑ Sleepwear/loungewear

Money

- ❑ Debit card(s)
- ❑ Credit card(s)
- ❑ Hard cash (US $100-200)
- ❑ Money belt

Documents

- ❑ Passport
- ❑ Other required ID: Vaccine card, entry visa, etc.
- ❑ Driver's license, student ID, hostel card, etc.
- ❑ Tickets & confirmations: flights, hotels, trains, rail pass, car rental, sight entries
- ❑ Photocopies of important documents
- ❑ Insurance details
- ❑ Guidebooks & maps
- ❑ Extra passport photos
- ❑ Notepad & pen
- ❑ Journal

Toiletries

- ❑ Soap, shampoo, toothbrush, toothpaste, floss, deodorant, sunscreen, brush/comb, etc.
- ❑ Medicines & vitamins
- ❑ First-aid kit
- ❑ Glasses/contacts/sunglasses
- ❑ Face masks & hand sanitizer
- ❑ Sewing kit
- ❑ Packet of tissues (for WC)
- ❑ Earplugs

Electronics

- ❑ Mobile phone
- ❑ Camera & related gear
- ❑ Tablet/ebook reader/laptop
- ❑ Headphones/earbuds
- ❑ Chargers & batteries
- ❑ Plug adapters

Miscellaneous

- ❑ Day pack
- ❑ Sealable plastic baggies
- ❑ Laundry supplies
- ❑ Small umbrella
- ❑ Travel alarm/watch

Optional Extras

- ❑ Second pair of shoes
- ❑ Travel hairdryer
- ❑ Disinfecting wipes
- ❑ Water bottle
- ❑ Fold-up tote bag
- ❑ Small flashlight & binoculars
- ❑ Small towel or washcloth
- ❑ Tiny lock

Dutch Survival Phrases

Most locals speak English, but if you learn the pleasantries and key phrases, you'll connect better with the Dutch people. To pronounce the guttural Dutch "g" (indicated in phonetics by h), make a clear-your-throat sound, similar to the "ch" in the Scottish word "loch."

Hello. (informal)	Hallo.	**hah**-loh
Good day.	Dag.	da*h*
Good morning.	Goedemorgen.	**hoo**-deh-mor-*h*ehn
Do you speak English?	Spreekt u Engels?	shpraykt oo **eng**-ehls
Yes. / No.	Ja. / Nee.	yah / nay
I (don't) understand.	Ik begrijp (het niet).	ik beh-**h**ripe (heht neet)
Please. (can also mean "You're welcome")	Alstublieft. **ahl**-stoo-bleeft	
Thank you.	Dank u wel.	dahnk oo vehl
Excuse me.	Pardon.	**par**-dohn
Goodbye.	Tot ziens.	toht zeens
one / two / three	een / twee / drie	ayn / t'vay / dree
What does it cost?	Wat kost het?	vaht kohst heht
I'd like / We'd like...	Ik wil graag / Wij willen graag... ik vil *h*rah / vy **vil**-lehn *h*rah	
...a train / bus ticket to ____.	...een trein / bus kaartje naar ____. ayn trayn / boos **kart**-yeh nar ____	
...to rent a bike.	...een fiets huren.	ayn feets **hoo**-rehn
Where is...?	Waar is...?	var is
...the train / bus station	...het trein / bus station heht trayn / boos **staht**-see-ohn	
...the tourist info office	...de VVV	deh fay fay fay
...the toilet	...het toilet	heht **twah**-leht
men / women	mannen / vrouwen	**mah**-nehn / **frow**-ehn
left / right	links / rechts	links / re*h*ts
straight ahead	rechtdoor	re*h*t-dor
What time does this open / close?	Hoe laat gaat het open / dicht? hoo laht *h*aht heht **oh**-pehn / di*h*t	
today / tomorrow	vandaag / morgen	**fahn**-da*h* / **mor**-*h*ehn

In a Dutch Restaurant

The all-purpose Dutch word *alstublieft* (ahl-stoo-bleeft) means "please," but it can also mean "here you are" (when the server hands you something), "thanks" (when taking payment from you), or "you're welcome" (when handing you change).

I'd like / We'd like...	Ik will graag / Wij willen graag... ik vil *h*rah / vy **vil**-lehn *h*rah
...a table for one / two.	...een tafel voor een / twee. ayn **tah**-fehl for ayn / t'vay
...to reserve a table.	...een tafel reserveren. ayn **tah**-fehl **ray**-zehr-feh-rehn
...the menu (in English).	...het menu (in het Engels). heht meh-**noo** (in heht **eng**-ehls)
Is this table free?	Is deze tafel vrij? is **day**-zeh **tah**-fehl fry
to go	om mee te nemen ohm may teh **nay**-mehn
with / without	met / zonder meht / **zohn**-der
and / or	en / of ehn / of
breakfast / lunch / dinner	ontbijt / middagmaal / avondmaal **ohnt**-bite / **mid**-dah-mahl / **ah**-fohnd-mahl
bread / cheese / sandwich	brood / kaas / sandwich brohd / kahs / **sand**-vich
soup / salad	soep / sla soop / slah
meat / chicken / fish	vlees / kip / vis flays / kip / fis
fruit / vegetables	vrucht / groenten fru*h*t / *h*roon-tehn
dessert / pastries	gebak *h*eh-**bahk**
mineral water / tap water	mineraalwater / kraanwater min-eh-rahl-**vah**-ter / **krahn**-vah-ter
coffee / tea	koffie / thee **koh**-fee / tay
wine / beer	wijn / bier vine / beer
red / white	rode / witte **roh**-deh / **vit**-teh
glass / bottle	glas / fles *h*lahs / flehs
Cheers!	Proost! prohst
The bill, please.	De rekening, alstublieft. deh **ray**-keh-neeng ahl-stoo-bleeft
tip	fooi foy
Tasty.	Lekker. **leh**-ker

INDEX

Start your trip at

Our website enhances this book and turns

Explore Europe

At ricksteves.com you can browse through thousands of articles, videos, photos and radio interviews, plus find a wealth of money-saving travel tips for planning your dream trip. And with our mobile-friendly website, you can easily access all this great travel information anywhere you go.

TV Shows

Preview the places you'll visit by watching entire half-hour episodes of *Rick Steves' Europe* (choose from all 100 shows) on-demand, for free.

ricksteves.com

your travel dreams into affordable reality

Radio Interviews

Enjoy ready access to Rick's vast library of radio interviews covering travel tips and cultural insights that relate specifically to your Europe travel plans.

Travel Forums

Learn, ask, share! Our online community of savvy travelers is a great resource for first-time travelers to Europe, as well as seasoned pros.

Travel News

Subscribe to our free Travel News e-newsletter, and get monthly updates from Rick on what's happening in Europe.

Classroom Europe®

Check out our free resource for educators with 500 short video clips from the *Rick Steves' Europe* TV show.

Audio Europe™

Rick's Free Travel App

Get your FREE Rick Steves Audio Europe™ app to enjoy…

- Dozens of self-guided tours of Europe's top museums, sights and historic walks
- Hundreds of tracks filled with cultural insights and sightseeing tips from Rick's radio interviews
- All organized into handy geographic playlists
- For Apple and Android

With Rick whispering in your ear, Europe gets even better.

Find out more at ricksteves.com

Pack Light and Right

Gear up for your next adventure at ricksteves.com

Light Luggage

Pack light and right with Rick Steves' affordable, custom-designed rolling carry-on bags, backpacks, day packs and shoulder bags.

Accessories

From packing cubes to moneybelts and beyond, Rick has personally selected the travel goodies that will help your trip go smoother.

Shop at ricksteves.com

Rick Steves has

Experience maximum Europe

Save time and energy

This guidebook is your
independent-travel toolkit. But
for all it delivers, it's still up to you
to devote the time and energy it
takes to manage the preparation
and logistics that are essential for a
happy trip. If that's a hassle, there's
a solution.

Rick Steves Tours

A Rick Steves tour takes you to
Europe's most interesting places
with great guides and small groups.

great tours, too!

with minimum stress

We follow Rick's favorite itineraries, ride in comfy buses, stay in family-run hotels, and bring you intimately close to the Europe you've traveled so far to see. Most importantly, we take away the logistical headaches so you can focus on the fun.

Join the fun

This year we'll take thousands of free-spirited travelers—nearly half of them repeat customers—along with us on four dozen different itineraries, from Ireland to Italy to Athens. Is a Rick Steves tour the right fit for your travel dreams? Find out at ricksteves.com, where you can check seat availability and sign up.

Europe is best experienced with happy travel partners. We hope you can join us.

See our itineraries at ricksteves.com

A Guide for Every Trip

BEST OF GUIDES

Full-color guides in an easy-to-scan format, focusing on top sights and experiences in popular destinations

Best of England
Best of Europe
Best of France
Best of Germany

Best of Ireland
Best of Italy
Best of Scotland
Best of Spain

COMPREHENSIVE GUIDES

City, country, and regional guides printed on Bible-thin paper. Packed with detailed coverage for a multi-week trip exploring iconic sights and more

Amsterdam &
  the Netherlands
Barcelona
Belgium: Bruges, Brussels,
  Antwerp & Ghent
Berlin
Budapest
Central Europe
Croatia & Slovenia
England
Florence & Tuscany
France
Germany
Great Britain
Greece: Athens &
  the Peloponnese
Iceland

Ireland
Istanbul
Italy
London
Paris
Portugal
Prague & the Czech Republic
Provence & the French
  Riviera
Rome
Scandinavia
Scotland
Sicily
Spain
Switzerland
Venice
Vienna, Salzburg & Tirol

Many guides are available as ebooks.

POCKET GUIDES
Compact guides for shorter city trips

Amsterdam	Italy's Cinque Terre	Prague
Athens	London	Rome
Barcelona	Munich & Salzburg	Venice
Florence	Paris	Vienna

SNAPSHOT GUIDES
Focused single-destination coverage

Basque Country: Spain & France
Copenhagen & the Best of Denmark
Dublin
Dubrovnik
Edinburgh
Hill Towns of Central Italy
Krakow, Warsaw & Gdansk
Lisbon
Loire Valley
Madrid & Toledo
Milan & the Italian Lakes District
Naples & the Amalfi Coast
Nice & the French Riviera
Normandy
Northern Ireland
Norway
Reykjavík
Rothenburg & the Rhine
Sevilla, Granada & Southern Spain
St. Petersburg, Helsinki & Tallinn
Stockholm

CRUISE PORTS GUIDES
Reference for cruise ports of call

Mediterranean Cruise Ports
Scandinavian & Northern European
  Cruise Ports

TRAVEL SKILLS & CULTURE
Greater information and insight

Europe 101
Europe Through the Back Door
Europe's Top 100 Masterpieces
European Christmas
European Easter
European Festivals
For the Love of Europe
Italy for Food Lovers
Travel as a Political Act

PHRASE BOOKS & DICTIONARIES

French
French, Italian & German
German
Italian
Portuguese
Spanish

PLANNING MAPS

Britain, Ireland & London
Europe
France & Paris
Germany, Austria & Switzerland
Iceland
Ireland
Italy
Scotland
Spain & Portugal

PHOTO CREDITS

Avalon Travel
Hachette Book Group
1700 Fourth Street
Berkeley, CA 94710

Printed in China by RR Donnelley
Fourth Edition
First printing April 2024

ISBN 978-1-64171-589-8

For the latest on Rick's talks, guidebooks, tours, public television series, and public radio show, contact Rick Steves' Europe, 130 Fourth Avenue North, Edmonds, WA 98020, +1 425 771 8303, RickSteves.com, rick@ricksteves.com.

Rick Steves' Europe
Managing Editor: Jennifer Madison Davis
Editorial Group Manager: Cathy Lu
Editors: Glenn Eriksen, Tom Griffin, Suzanne Kotz, Rosie Leutzinger, Teresa Nemeth, Jessica Shaw, Carrie Shepherd, Chelsea Wing
Creative Director: Sandra Hundacker
Maps & Graphics: Orin Dubrow, David C. Hoerlein, Lauren Mills, Mary Rostad

Avalon Travel
Senior Editor and Series Manager: Madhu Prasher
Associate Managing Editors: Jamie Andrade, Sierra Machado
Copy Editor: Kelly Lydick
Proofreader: Jennifer Malnick
Indexer: Claire Splan
Production & Typesetting: Christine DeLorenzo, Jane Musser
Cover Design: Kimberly Glyder Design
Interior Design: Rue Flaherty
Maps & Graphics: Kat Bennett, Lohnes + Wright

Let's Keep on Travelin'

Your trip doesn't need to end.

Follow Rick on social media!